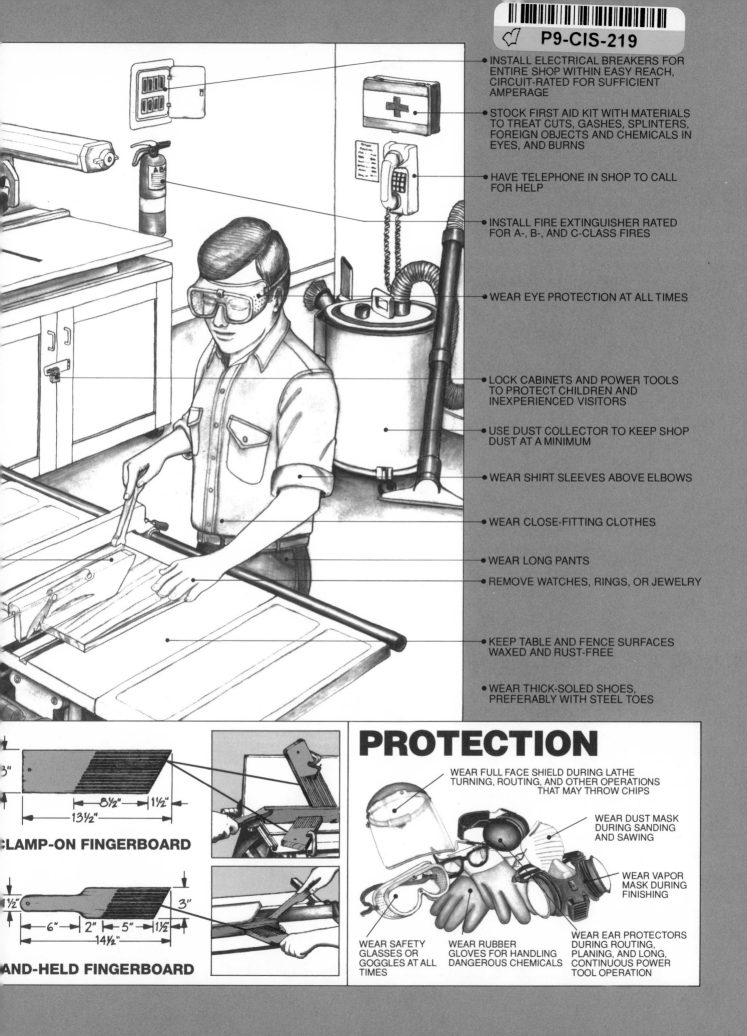

- INSTALL ELECTRICAL BREAKERS FOR ENTIRE SHOP WITHIN EASY REACH, CIRCUIT-RATED FOR SUFFICIENT AMPERAGE
- STOCK FIRST AID KIT WITH MATERIALS TO TREAT CUTS, GASHES, SPLINTERS, FOREIGN OBJECTS AND CHEMICALS IN EYES, AND BURNS
- HAVE TELEPHONE IN SHOP TO CALL FOR HELP
- INSTALL FIRE EXTINGUISHER RATED FOR A-, B-, AND C-CLASS FIRES
- WEAR EYE PROTECTION AT ALL TIMES
- LOCK CABINETS AND POWER TOOLS TO PROTECT CHILDREN AND INEXPERIENCED VISITORS
- USE DUST COLLECTOR TO KEEP SHOP DUST AT A MINIMUM
- WEAR SHIRT SLEEVES ABOVE ELBOWS
- WEAR CLOSE-FITTING CLOTHES
- WEAR LONG PANTS
- REMOVE WATCHES, RINGS, OR JEWELRY
- KEEP TABLE AND FENCE SURFACES WAXED AND RUST-FREE
- WEAR THICK-SOLED SHOES, PREFERABLY WITH STEEL TOES

3"
8½" 1½"
13½"

CLAMP-ON FINGERBOARD

1½" 3"
6" 2" 5" 1½"
14½"

AND-HELD FINGERBOARD

PROTECTION

WEAR FULL FACE SHIELD DURING LATHE TURNING, ROUTING, AND OTHER OPERATIONS THAT MAY THROW CHIPS

WEAR DUST MASK DURING SANDING AND SAWING

WEAR VAPOR MASK DURING FINISHING

WEAR SAFETY GLASSES OR GOGGLES AT ALL TIMES

WEAR RUBBER GLOVES FOR HANDLING DANGEROUS CHEMICALS

WEAR EAR PROTECTORS DURING ROUTING, PLANING, AND LONG, CONTINUOUS POWER TOOL OPERATION

THE WORKSHOP COMPANION®

MAKING JIGS AND FIXTURES

TECHNIQUES FOR BETTER WOODWORKING

by Nick Engler

Rodale Press
Emmaus, Pennsylvania

Printed in the United States of America on acid-free ∞, recycled ♲ paper

If you have any questions or comments concerning this book, please write:
Rodale Press
Book Readers' Service
33 East Minor Street
Emmaus, PA 18098

About the Author: Nick Engler is an experienced woodworker, writer, teacher, and inventor. He worked as a luthier for many years, making traditional American musical instruments before he founded *Hands On!* magazine. He has taught at the University of Cincinnati and gives woodworking seminars around the country. He contributes to woodworking magazines and designs tools for America's Best Tool Company. This is his forty-third book.

Series Editor: Kevin Ireland
Editors: Ken Burton
         Roger Yepsen
Copy Editor: Sarah Dunn
Graphic Designer: Linda Watts
Illustrator: Mary Jane Favorite
Master Craftsman: Jim McCann
Photographer: Karen Callahan
Cover Photographer: Mitch Mandel
Proofreader: Hue Park
Indexer: Beverly Bremer
Interior and endpaper illustrations by Mary Jane Favorite
Produced by Bookworks, Inc., West Milton, Ohio

Library of Congress Cataloging-in-Publication Data

Engler, Nick.
    Making jigs and fixtures/by Nick Engler.
        p.   cm. — (Workshop companion)
    Includes index.
    ISBN 0–87596–689–6 (hardcover: alk. paper)
    1. Woodworking tools — Design and construction.
    2. Woodwork — Equipment and supplies — Design
    and construction. 3. Jigs and fixtures — Design and
    construction. I. Title. II. Series: Engler, Nick.
    Workshop companion.
TT186.E5   1995
684'.08'028 — dc20   95–249

    6 8 10 9 7   hardcover

The author and editors who compiled this book have tried to make all the contents as accurate and as correct as possible. Plans, illustrations, photographs, and text have all been carefully checked and cross-checked. However, due to the variability of local conditions, construction materials, personal skill, and so on, neither the author nor Rodale Press assumes any responsibility for any injuries suffered, or for damages or other losses incurred that result from the material presented herein. All instructions and plans should be carefully studied and clearly understood before beginning construction.

Patent Notice
Many of the jigs and fixtures shown in this book are patented, patent pending, or include patented features. Readers are encouraged to make a single copy of each for their personal use or for a gift. However, manufacture for sale or profit is forbidden without the written permission of the patent owner, America's Best Tool Company, Inc.

Special Thanks to:

America's Best Tool Company, Inc.
West Milton, Ohio

CMT Tools
Oldsmar, Florida

Quality VAKuum Products
Concord, Massachusetts

Carlo Venditto
Clearwater, Florida

Wertz Hardware
West Milton, Ohio

CONTENTS

TECHNIQUES

1. A Jig-Making Primer   2

    Designing Jigs and Fixtures   3

    Jig-Making Materials and Methods   7

        Jig-Making Materials   8

        Common Jig and Fixture Assemblies   11

        Holes, Counterbores, and Slots   15

2. Safety and Dust Collection   18

    Keeping Out of Danger   19

    Controlling Dust   22

        Selecting a Dust Collector   26

3. Support and Guidance   27

    Support: Tables and Work Surfaces   28

    Guidance: Fences and Straightedges   32

    Guides for Cutting Curves, Contours, and Holes   34

4. Measuring and Positioning   38

    Measurement and Layout   39

    Positioning the Workpiece   42

        Incremental Positioning   45

5. **Clamping and Assembling**   47

    Clamps   48

       Vacuum Clamps   54

    Special Holding Jigs   57

    Assembly Jigs   59

PROJECTS

6. **A Craftsman's Dozen:**
12 Jigs and Fixtures You Cannot Work Without   62

    1. Pusher   63

    2. Auxiliary Fence   65

    3. Universal Featherboard   69

    4. Support Stand   73

    5. Adjustable-Height Fence   80

    6. Tenoning Jig   84

    7. Sliding Cutoff Table   89

    8. Lift-Top Router Table   98

    9. Router Height Adjustor   109

    10. Tilting Drill Press Table   111

    11. Circular Saw Guide   117

    12. Knock-Down Cutting Grid   121

Index 124

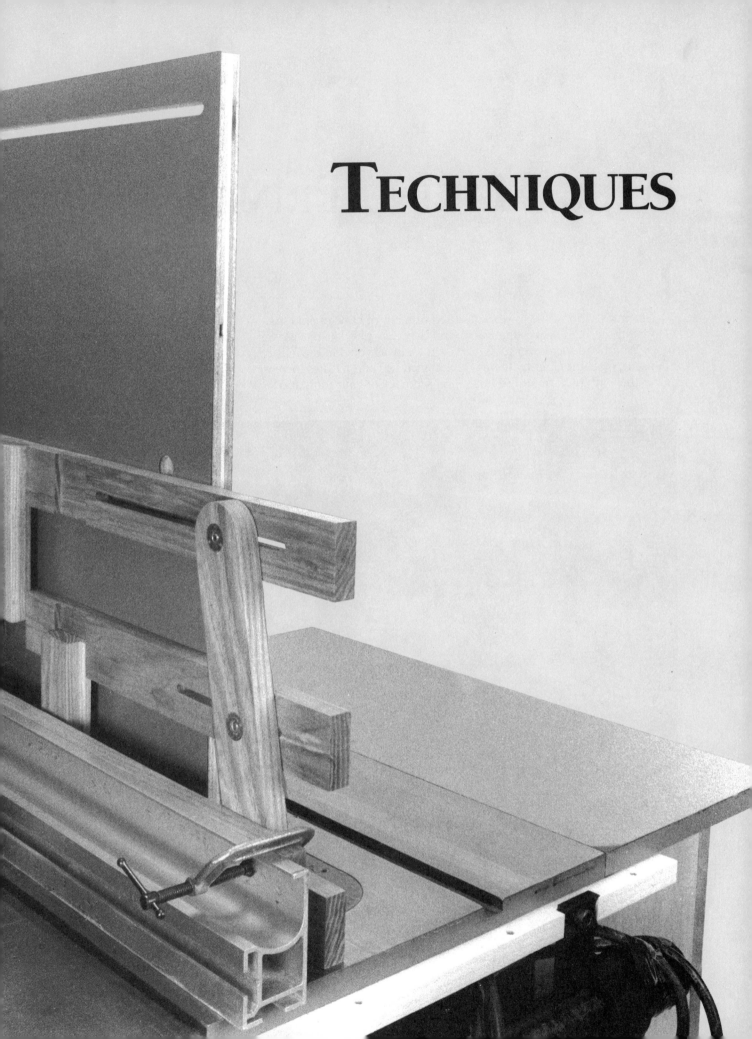

TECHNIQUES

1

A JIG-MAKING PRIMER

I t's almost impossible to work wood without making jigs and fixtures. Woodworking power tools are useful machines, but by themselves they will perform only a limited number of basic operations — and they may not do these as well or as easily as you'd like. Well-designed jigs and fixtures increase the accuracy of your tools and make them easier and safer to use. They also extend their capabilities, allowing you to perform a wider range of woodworking operations.

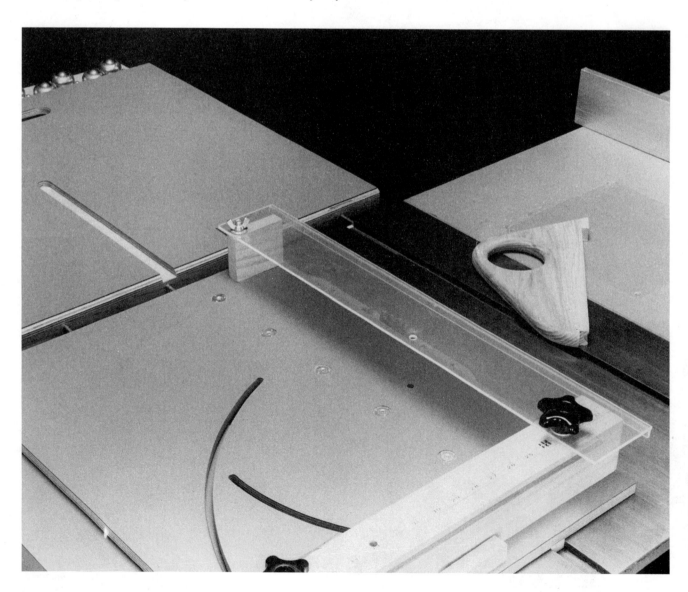

DESIGNING JIGS AND FIXTURES

You don't have to be a trained engineer to build effective jigs and fixtures, but it helps to think like one. Before you start, form a clear idea in your mind of what you want the jig to do. Don't be too ambitious; a jig must not overextend your tools — or you. As you design the jig, follow three simple rules of thumb:

■ Make it *simple to build*. If the design is too complex, it often isn't worth the effort.

■ Make it *as accurate as possible*. As long as you choose the right materials and methods, you can build a precision tool with ordinary workshop equipment.

■ Make it *safe to use*. When properly designed, a jig should increase the safety of a woodworking operation.

SIMPLICITY

In 25 years of woodworking, I've found that simple jigs always work best. Most of the complex monsters I built were disappointments. The reason is obvious: The more complex the machine (and jigs are machines), the more that can go wrong.

To keep your jigs and fixtures simple:

■ Use as few parts as possible. Make sure that every part in your design has a good reason for being there. (*SEE FIGURE 1-1.*)

■ Build jigs with flat surfaces and square corners. Although many woodworking machines will create a range of curves and angles, what they do best is plane flat surfaces, joint square edges, and cut in a straight line. Design your jigs to take advantage of this. (*SEE FIGURE 1-2.*)

■ Don't try to make a jig perform too many operations unless it will perform them simply. It's one thing to try to make a jig as capable as possible, but if it starts accumulating parts and hardware until the design looks like a spaceship, set your sights a little lower. (*SEE FIGURE 1-3.*)

1-1 This *overhead routing jig* holds a router stationary above the workpiece, allowing you to pin-rout patterns, cut flutes and reeds in spindles, and create wooden signs. There are just nine parts, counting the plastic mounting plate — you can knock it together in about an hour. But it greatly extends the capabilities of your router.

1-2 The parts of the overhead routing jig are rectangular in shape, assembled with butt joints. The assembly that holds the router is a simple box with a transparent bottom, supported by two 90-degree brackets. Straight edges and square assemblies not only make the jig easier to build, they make it easier to build *accurately*.

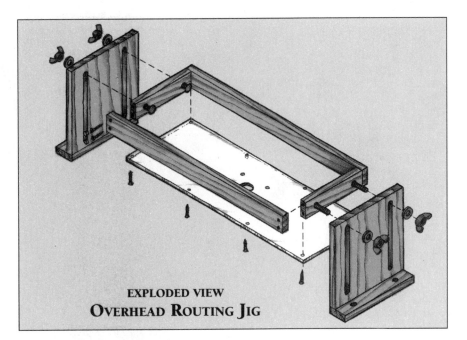

EXPLODED VIEW
OVERHEAD ROUTING JIG

1-3 This multipurpose routing jig evolved directly from the overhead routing jig. By lengthening the supports and adding a fence, the jig not only serves as an overhead router, it also converts to make a small, portable router table. This doubles its usefulness without making it overly complex.

ACCURACY

Simple jigs also tend to be more precise. In mechanical engineering, there is a phenomenon known as *tolerance stack-up*. A good woodworker can cut a part to within 1/64 inch of the desired dimension. But if there are 64 parts in an assembly, then the last part is liable to be as much as 1 inch off the mark when you put them all together. If you use fewer parts, you can work to tighter tolerances.

You also can increase accuracy by making the key parts of your jig *adjustable*. If it's important that a fence be fixed at a certain angle, mount it in such a way that you can adjust it a few degrees one way or the other. If a stop has to hold a workpiece in a certain place, attach the stop so you can adjust its position. (*See Figure 1-4.*)

Sawdust is one of the most common causes of inaccuracy in woodworking. It accumulates on worktables, fences, and faces, keeps the work from contacting these surfaces, and holds the work in the wrong position. When you design a jig, give the sawdust someplace to go — into channels and open spaces. Where possible, provide dust collection. (*See Figure 1-5.*)

Finally, accuracy depends on your work habits when you build the jig. Think each procedure through, make sure your tools are properly aligned, check and double-check your measurements. Refer to "Construction Methods" on page 12 for some helpful tips.

1-4 The mounting holes in the fence on this *cutoff jig* are slightly larger in diameter than the bolts that hold it in place. This allows you to adjust the angle of the fence a few degrees right and left to align it perfectly square to the blade.

HOLE SLIGHTLY LARGER THAN BOLT

1-5 The clamp-on *stop* shown has double-mitered edges to limit the effects of sawdust on its accuracy. An ordinary stop has flat edges. The sawdust piles up against them, preventing the workpiece from butting against the stop. Consequently, the cut you're making may not be precise. When using this stop, however, the sawdust piles up in the spaces behind the point of the miter, the workpiece contacts the stop, and the cut remains accurate.

SAFETY

To design a safe jig, think through the operation you want it to perform:

■ Will the cutter and the workpiece be secure throughout the entire procedure? Do you need to build a carriage for the workpiece or clamp it to the jig? (*See Figure 1-6.*)

■ Will the blade or the cutter be exposed during the operation? Should you cover it with a guard or rearrange the components of the jig to cover it? (*See Figure 1-7.*)

1-6 This *splined miter jig* enables you to safely perform an operation that otherwise would be dangerous and imprecise. The jig is a simple carriage that rides along the table saw fence and past the blade, holding the workpiece 45 degrees to the work surface. It would be extremely difficult to hold the board steady at that angle with your hands alone.

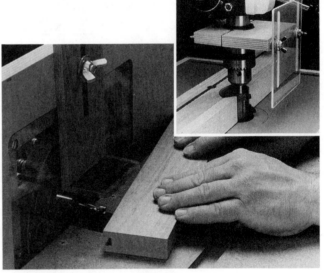

1-7 Never design a jig that com-pletely exposes the cutter. Always "bury" as much of the cutter as possible in the jig, and — if possible — protect yourself from the exposed portion with a guard. For example, when using this *joint-making jig,* the router is held horizontally so the unused portion of the bit is behind the mounting plate. In the routing setup for the drill press, part of the bit is buried in the fence. In both cases, a guard helps protect you from the exposed portion of the cutter.

■ Where will your fingers (and the rest of your body) be during the operation? Is it possible that they might stray inside the danger zone? Can you add handles, knobs, or holding devices to prevent this? (SEE FIGURE 1-8.)

■ Could the workpiece kick back? Should you use a clamp or a backstop to prevent this? If it does kick back, where will your body be? Can you design the jig so your body will always be out of the line of fire? (SEE FIGURE 1-9.)

■ Where will the cutter throw chips and sawdust during the operation? Can you provide dust collection to keep this to a minimum? Do you need to add a deflector or a shield to protect you or to make it more comfortable to work? Refer to "Controlling Dust" on page 22 for more information.

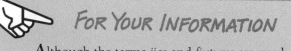

FOR YOUR INFORMATION

Although the terms *jigs* and *fixtures* are used interchangeably by woodworkers, there is a difference. Technically, a jig holds and guides a cutting tool, while a fixture holds and guides a workpiece.

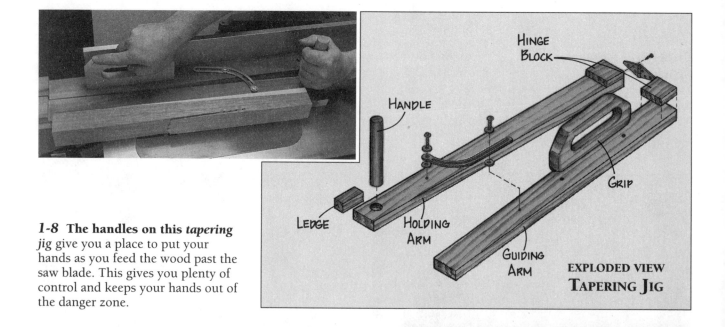

1-8 The handles on this *tapering* *jig* give you a place to put your hands as you feed the wood past the saw blade. This gives you plenty of control and keeps your hands out of the danger zone.

1-9 This extra-long *miter gauge* *extension* keeps long boards at the proper angle to the saw blade. If you attach it to the miter gauge so it passes over the blade, providing a backstop for the wood on *both* sides of the cut, it will also prevent kickback. Should the saw blade catch on either portion of the cut-off board, the extension will keep it from pitching wood at you.

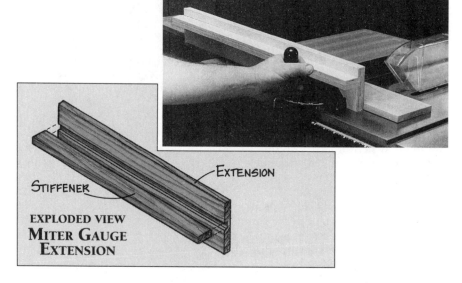

JIG-MAKING MATERIALS AND METHODS

CHOOSING MATERIALS

When making a jig or a fixture, you must understand the properties of the materials you're working with. The completed accessory should be strong enough to do the job, durable enough to stand up to repeated use, and stable enough to hold a setting or remain in alignment indefinitely. Consequently, you must choose your materials for strength, durability, and stability. And don't try to make every part from the same material. Each part has different requirements; consequently, many successful jigs are blends of wood, plywood, particleboard, and plastic.

WOOD

Of all the jig-making materials, wood is the strongest but the least stable—its strength and stability depend on the grain direction. Wood is strong *along* the grain and weak *across* the grain. It's almost completely stable *along* the grain, but it expands and contracts *across* the grain. When using it in a jig, you must carefully arrange the wood grain to get the strength and stability you need.

Some woods are better suited for jig making than others. You want to pick woods that are strong, durable, as stable as possible, and easily machined to a smooth surface. The traditional favorite is *hard maple*. This light-colored, closed-grain wood is strong and dense, and it machines well, although it's not particularly stable. *Birch* is another common choice, although it's more difficult to machine than maple and prone to distort. My own favorites are *ash* and *poplar*. Both are softer and less dense than maple, but they are still sufficiently strong and durable. They also expand and contract less and are easier to machine. Better yet, they're less expensive than maple.

When you need an extremely hard, durable wood, *beech, hickory,* and *fruitwood* (especially pear) are good choices. Also consider exotic imported woods such as *rosewood, cocobolo, bocote,* and *teak*. Many imports are more stable than most domestics. Teak, for example, moves less than half as much as maple.

PLYWOOD

Plywood is not as strong as wood. It will not support as much load as wood will along the grain. However, it is just as durable and much more stable. Two types are suitable for jig making: *hardwood plywood* and *European birch plywood*. Cabinet-grade (A-2 or 1-2) hardwood plywood is made up of several thick layers of an inexpensive hardwood (usually poplar) covered with two thin layers of a "face-grade" hardwood veneer (such as birch or oak). It's a good utility material for structural pieces, but it's not stable enough for parts that must remain perfectly flat. For these, use European birch plywood, which includes Baltic Birch and Apple-ply. This material is glued up from many thin layers of birch or another closed-grain hardwood, all exactly the same thickness and density. This makes it much more stable than other types of plywood.

PARTICLEBOARD

Particleboard is the weakest and least durable of commonly used jig-making materials, but it's also the most stable. Ordinary 1-M-2 particleboard (made from sawdust-size wood particles) is useful for building patterns and forms. If you cover it with plastic laminate to increase the durability of the surface and brace it with wood or plywood to increase its strength, it makes excellent work surfaces. *Sink cutouts,* which you can buy at many building supply centers for a few dollars, are 1-M-2 particleboard covered with plastic laminate. *Tempered hardboard* is made from extremely small particles mixed with resins. It's commonly available in ⅛- and ¼-inch thicknesses, and makes good inserts and templates. *Medium-density fiberboard (MDF)* is a similar material, but it comes in thicker sheets. MDF is heavier and not as readily available as ordinary particleboard, but it's more stable and easier to machine, produces a smoother surface, and remains flatter. MDF is my favorite for making work surfaces.

A BIT OF ADVICE

If you work with tropical woods, purchase them from a responsible supplier who respects the sensitive environments of these rain forests from which they come. For a list of suppliers, ask for the "Good Wood" list from:

Woodworker's Alliance for Rainforest Protection
Box 133
Coos Bay, OR 97420

JIG-MAKING MATERIALS

MATERIAL	STRENGTH	DURABILITY	STABILITY	SPECIAL PROPERTIES	COMMON USES
WOOD					
Domestic hardwoods (maple, birch, ash, poplar)	High along the grain	High	Low across the grain	Strong and stable along the wood grain; machines easily	Structural parts that require strength and stability in one direction only
Exotic imports (rosewood, cocobolo, bocote, teak)	High along the grain	Very high	Medium across the grain	Strong and stable along the wood grain; decorative; water resistant	Handles, grips, knobs, other frequently handled parts
PLYWOOD					
Hardwood plywood	Medium	Medium-high	Medium	Thin face veneers	Structural parts
European plywood	Medium-high	High	Medium-high	Thick face veneers; easy to machine	Parts requiring extra strength or stability
PARTICLEBOARD					
1-M-2 particleboard	Low	Medium	Medium	Chips easily; difficult to machine	Templates, forms, patterns, work surfaces
Tempered hardboard	Low	Medium-high	High	Hard surface; limited thicknesses	Templates, inserts
Medium-density fiberboard	Low	Medium	High	Easy to machine; remains flat	Templates, forms, patterns, work surfaces
PLASTICS					
Acrylics	Medium	High	Very high	Rigid; available in clear or opaque sheets	Patterns, guards, mounting plates
Polycarbonates	Medium	High	Very high	Flexible; available in clear or opaque sheets	Patterns, guards
UHMW	Medium	Very high	Very high	Flexible; slippery; long-wearing; easy to machine	Runners, guides, moving parts
Phenolics	Medium	Very high	Very high	Rigid; long-wearing	Runners, parts that must not flex
Plastic laminates	Low	High	Very high	Available in thin sheets only	Covering for work surfaces and fences

FOR BEST RESULTS

To keep a laminate-covered particleboard or MDF work surface perfectly flat, apply plastic laminate to *both* faces. Or, coat the uncovered face with enamel paint or polyurethane immediately. That way, both faces will absorb and release moisture at the same rate. If you leave one face uncovered and untreated, it will expand and contract faster than the covered face, and the work surface will cup.

PLASTICS

There are five types of plastics used in jig making that can be readily machined with woodworking tools. *Acrylics,* such as Plexiglas, are strong and rigid but somewhat brittle. They come in different thicknesses and are available in many colors, both opaque and transparent. Acrylics are useful for templates and guards. In thicknesses of ⅜ inch or more, they make good mounting plates. *Polycarbonates,* such as Lexan, have properties similar to acrylics, but they are less brittle and not as rigid. Consequently, they flex too much to be used for mounting plates, but are useful for making guards and templates. *Ultrahigh–molecular weight plastics (UHMW)* are dense, smooth, and slippery. They also are somewhat elastic and wear like iron. Consequently, they are a good choice for moving parts, runners, slides, and templates, as long as a small amount of flexibility does not adversely affect the operation of the jig. If you need more rigidity, use *phenolics.* Although they are not as smooth or slippery as UHMW, they are just as long-wearing. They are also extremely strong, resistant to heat, and impervious to most workshop chemicals. Finally, *plastic laminates* such as Formica are useful for covering work surfaces and fences to make them more durable and to reduce friction. These are made from layers of paper sandwiched together with phenolic resin.

CHOOSING HARDWARE

Because jigs and fixtures are tools, often with moving parts, they are liable to use more hardware than your average woodworking project. They also require a greater variety of hardware.

FASTENERS

Most structural parts of jigs and fixtures are permanently assembled with glue, screws, and nails, as you might expect. Some parts, however, are attached temporarily to make them interchangeable, adjustable, or easier to store. There are many different types of *knock-down* fasteners to choose from to attach a part temporarily. The most common choices are threaded fasteners, such as *machine screws, carriage bolts,* and *hex bolts,* which are driven through the wood and secured with *hex nuts.* To create a superlong bolt, cut a *threaded rod* (also known as all-thread) to the length required. To imbed nuts in the wood, use *T-nuts* or *threaded inserts.*

WHERE TO FIND IT

All of the jig-making materials mentioned can be purchased locally or ordered through the mail. If you cannot find a particular wood or wood product at a lumberyard or building supply center, they may be able to special-order it for you. If you have trouble finding specific hardwoods, European birch, or MDF, write or call:

Paxton Hardwoods
7455 Dawson Road
Cincinnati, OH 45243
(800) 325-9800

or

Woodcraft Supply Corp.
210 Wood County Industrial Park
P.O. Box 1686
Parkersburg, WV 26102
(800) 225-1153

You can buy plastic laminate through most cabinetmaking shops and building supply centers. Other plastics are available from suppliers that specialize in these materials. Look in your local phone book under "Plastics." You can also purchase some types of plastic from mail-order woodworking suppliers, such as Woodcraft, or from:

Woodworker's Supply, Inc.
1108 North Glenn Road
Casper, WY 82601
(800) 648-3953

FOR BEST RESULTS

Assemble plywood parts with *sheet metal screws* rather than wood screws. Sheet metal screws have threads the entire length of the shaft and are less likely to split the plies.

WING NUTS, THUMBSCREWS, AND KNOBS

To lock down a part securely and then release it without the benefit of a wrench or a screwdriver, use *wing nuts* and *thumbscrews* — you can turn these by hand. You can also turn *T-knobs, star knobs,* and *ratchet handles* in the same manner. *(See Figure 1-10.)*

CLAMPS AND HOLD-DOWNS

To hold a workpiece in a jig, use a clamp or a hold-down. You can make these devices from bolts, wing nuts, and knobs (as shown in "Clamps" on page 48), or you can purchase ready-made clamps. There are several types of *toggle clamps* manufactured especially for jig making. *(See Figure 1-11.)*

HINGES AND PIVOTS

If you need a part to tilt or swing, you can usually employ a simple *butt hinge* or *strap hinge*. For heavy parts or parts that will see a lot of service, use a *piano hinge*. If a hinge won't do, a hex bolt or a carriage bolt makes an excellent pivot. To secure a pivot bolt, use a pair of *jamb nuts* or a *stop nut*. These won't work themselves loose as the part pivots.

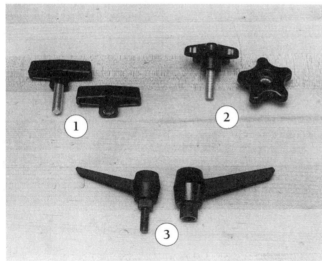

1-10 Fasteners such as *T-knobs* (1), *star knobs* (2), and *ratchet handles* (3) can be tightened and loosened by hand. Each type of knob is available with threaded inserts (so they can be used like large wing nuts) or threaded studs (so they can be used like large thumbscrews). Use T-knobs when you require a medium amount of pressure, and star knobs when you need to apply more. Ratchet handles are designed to work in tight spaces where you can't get a good grip on a T-knob or a star knob.

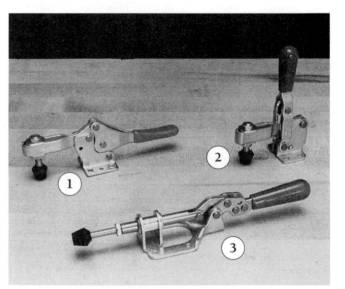

1-11 There are several types of toggle clamps available, although they do approximately the same thing. A *horizontal-handle toggle clamp* (1) applies pressure when you push down on the handle and locks when the handle is horizontal. A *vertical-handle toggle clamp* (2) applies pressure as you raise the handle and locks when the handle is vertical. An *in-line toggle clamp* (3) applies pressure in the direction that you throw the handle.

COMMON JIG AND FIXTURE ASSEMBLIES

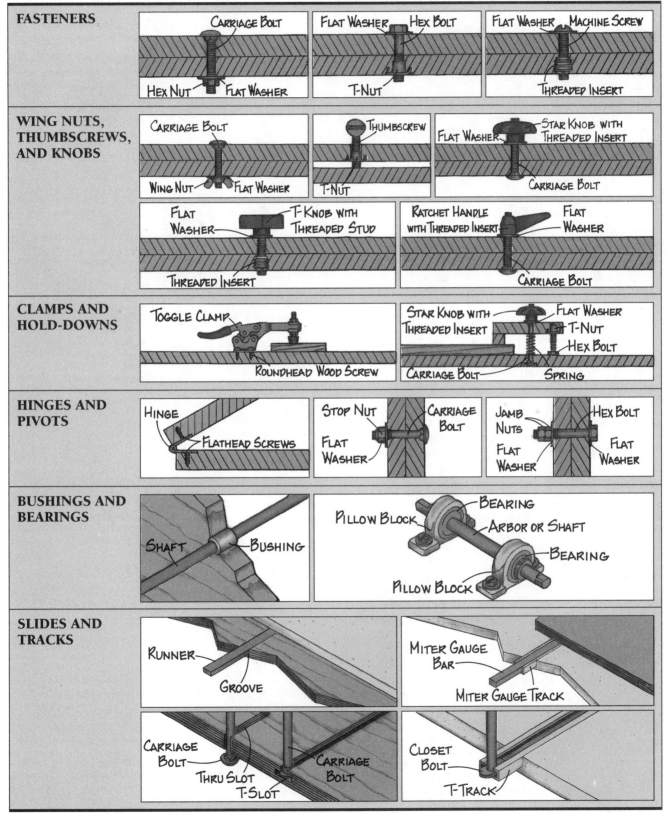

FASTENERS

CARRIAGE BOLT
HEX NUT · FLAT WASHER

FLAT WASHER — HEX BOLT
T-NUT

FLAT WASHER — MACHINE SCREW
THREADED INSERT

WING NUTS, THUMBSCREWS, AND KNOBS

CARRIAGE BOLT
WING NUT · FLAT WASHER

THUMBSCREW
T-NUT

FLAT WASHER · STAR KNOB WITH THREADED INSERT
CARRIAGE BOLT

FLAT WASHER — T-KNOB WITH THREADED STUD
THREADED INSERT

RATCHET HANDLE WITH THREADED INSERT · FLAT WASHER
CARRIAGE BOLT

CLAMPS AND HOLD-DOWNS

TOGGLE CLAMP
ROUNDHEAD WOOD SCREW

STAR KNOB WITH THREADED INSERT · FLAT WASHER
T-NUT
HEX BOLT
CARRIAGE BOLT · SPRING

HINGES AND PIVOTS

HINGE
FLATHEAD SCREWS

STOP NUT · CARRIAGE BOLT
FLAT WASHER

JAMB NUTS · HEX BOLT
FLAT WASHER
FLAT WASHER

BUSHINGS AND BEARINGS

SHAFT · BUSHING

PILLOW BLOCK · BEARING
ARBOR OR SHAFT
BEARING
PILLOW BLOCK

SLIDES AND TRACKS

RUNNER
GROOVE

MITER GAUGE BAR
MITER GAUGE TRACK

CARRIAGE BOLT
THRU SLOT
T-SLOT
CARRIAGE BOLT

CLOSET BOLT
T-TRACK

When selecting bolts to make pivots, make sure that the portion of the bolt inside the pivot hole is mostly *unthreaded*. Otherwise, the threads will eat away at the wood every time the part moves, enlarging the hole. In many cases, you will have to purchase a much longer bolt than you would otherwise need and cut away some of the threaded portion.

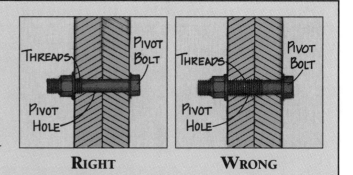

RIGHT   **WRONG**

BUSHINGS AND BEARINGS

When a pivot sees a lot of use, install a metal *bushing* inside the pivot hole to keep the wood from wearing away. Bushings are also needed where rotating metal *shafts* and *arbors* are mounted in wooden parts. If the shaft rotates constantly or at a high speed, use *ball bearings* mounted in *pillow blocks* to mount it.

SLIDES AND TRACKS

Sliding parts travel back and forth in grooves and slots, guided by hardware. For example, you can mount a sliding table on a *runner* or a metal *miter gauge bar* to follow a groove in a work surface. To lock down a sliding fence, you can fasten it in a slot with carriage bolts or *flange bolts* (also called *closet bolts*). If you cannot cut the slot completely through the jig, you'll have to make a *T-slot* to fit the heads and the shafts of the bolts. If the sliding mechanism will see a lot of use, consider using a metal *miter gauge track* or *T-track* instead of cutting a groove or a slot in the wood. (*SEE FIGURE 1-12.*)

You can purchase special jig-making hardware from most mail-order woodworking suppliers, including:

The Woodworkers' Store
4365 Willow Drive
Medina, MN 55340
(800) 279-4441

or

Eagle America, Inc.
124 Parker Court
P.O. Box 1099
Chardon, OH 44024
(800) 872-2511

1-12 Metal tracks wear better than slots and grooves cut in wood. They can also simplify a jig — in many cases, it's easier to install metal tracks than it is to rout a T-slot or a close-fitting groove for a runner. Simply screw the track to the wood. Or, if you want the top of the track even with the surface, cut a groove and screw the track into the bottom of the groove. The miter gauge track shown even lets you adjust the fit — tighten or loosen the screws that hold it to the wood until the runner slides smoothly but with minimum side-to-side play.

CONSTRUCTION METHODS

Most of the techniques required to build jigs and fixtures are the same as those used to build any woodworking project. However, there is a unique emphasis in jig making. The joinery is usually very simple — many jigs and fixtures are assembled with simple butt joints reinforced with fasteners. But the parts *and* the assembly must be extremely accurate for the jig to work properly — the parts must be cut to precise dimensions and angles, and the assembly must be flat, straight, and square. A few tips will help you achieve the necessary accuracy.

■ Before you start building, check the alignment of the tools you'll be using. For example, is the table saw blade square to the table? The miter gauge square to the blade? And don't just check the tools — make some test cuts and check the results. (*See Figures 1-13 and 1-14.*)

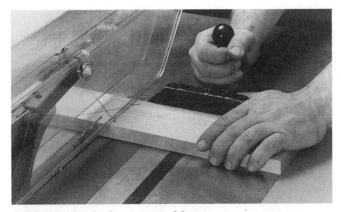

1-13 To check that your table saw is making a square cut, select a long, straight scrap and rip it so both edges are parallel. Mark an X near the center of the scrap, then cut through the X, using the miter gauge to guide the wood. To test the *miter gauge,* rest the scrap on a *face* as you cut. To check the *blade angle,* make the cut with the scrap held on edge.

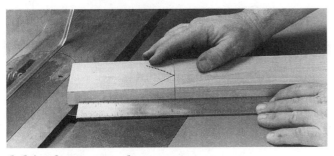

1-14 After cutting the scrap in two, turn one piece over so half of the X faces in the opposite direction. Butt the cut ends together and lay a straightedge against the edge. If the seam between the pieces gaps at the top or bottom, the saw is not making a square cut. Readjust the miter gauge or the blade and test it again. When the seam is tight, the cut is perfectly square.

■ Make sure *all* your materials are acclimated to your shop environment. Bring the wood and wood products inside and let them sit for a week or two while they reach equilibrium with the relative humidity in the shop. If you cut into them before they've had a chance to "shop-dry," the wood may be in motion — expanding or contracting as it absorbs or releases moisture. This, in turn, will affect the accuracy of your assembly. **Note:** Shop drying is necessary for plywood and particleboard as well as solid wood. These materials expand and contract also, although to a lesser degree.

■ Cut the wood parts slightly oversize while the boards are still rough — *before* you plane them. This will help to relieve any internal tension in the wood. Joint a face and an edge of each board to remove any cup or bow. Then plane and cut the boards to size.

■ Lay out your cuts with a loupe, magnifying lamp, or headband magnifier, even if you have good eyesight. You'll be surprised how much this improves the accuracy of your layouts. (*See Figure 1-15.*)

■ Always make test cuts before cutting good stock. Measure the results with a caliper or another precision measuring instrument, and adjust your setup until the results are literally within a hair's width of where you

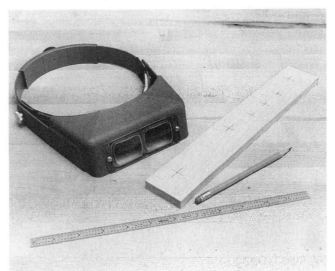

1-15 Use precision rules, squares, protractors, and a *headband magnifier* or another magnifying device when laying out jig parts. This makes it much easier to see tiny fractions of inches and degrees, even if you have good eyesight. Once you get used to the magnifier, you'll wonder how you ever did without it.

want them. It takes a little extra time to make cuts this accurate, but the results show on the completed jigs. (*See Figure 1-16.*)

■ Use corner clamps or brackets to keep parts square when fitting them and drilling screw or bolt holes. (*See Figure 1-17.*)

■ Test fit the parts and check their alignment before you glue them up. Remake any parts that won't align or fit properly.

■ Sand the surfaces with a stationary belt sander or disc sander to keep them flat and square. You can also make a simple jig to sand surfaces square to one another. (*See Figure 1-18.*) **Note:** If the overall dimensions of the assembly are important, build it about ¹⁄₆₄ inch oversize to allow for sanding.

■ Finish your jigs with a penetrating oil such as tung oil. A penetrating finish hardens the surface of wood and wood products by as much as 40 percent, making them much more durable. Apply at least two coats, then rub out the finish with an abrasive pad (such as Scotch-Brite) and paste wax. The abrasive will create an ultrasmooth surface, and the wax will lubricate and protect it.

TRY THIS TRICK

Mix 2 tablespoons of spar varnish and 1 cup of tung oil to make an extremely durable wipe-on penetrating finish for jigs.

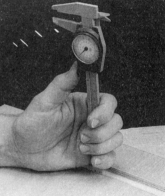

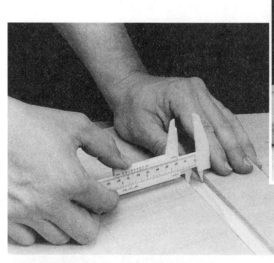

1-16 Use precision equipment to measure the results of your machine setups. A good *vernier caliper* (left) or *dial caliper* (right) is extremely useful for measuring test cuts and will help you refine your setups to within a few thousandths of an inch when you need extreme accuracy. Most models make both inside and outside measurements as well as probe the depths of holes, mortises, and other joints.

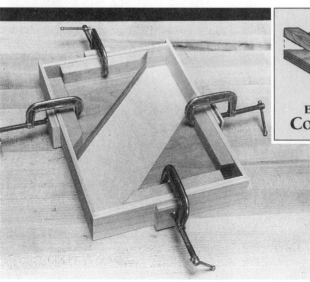

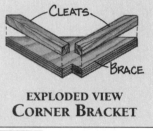

EXPLODED VIEW
CORNER BRACKET

1-17 It's not enough to lay out and cut the parts accurately; you must also assemble them accurately. Clamp the parts together *without* glue before drilling screw holes. Use corner clamps or brackets (shown) to align the corners and hold them absolutely square as you assemble and clamp the parts. **Note:** The notches in the brackets prevent them from contacting any glue that squeezes out of the corner joint.

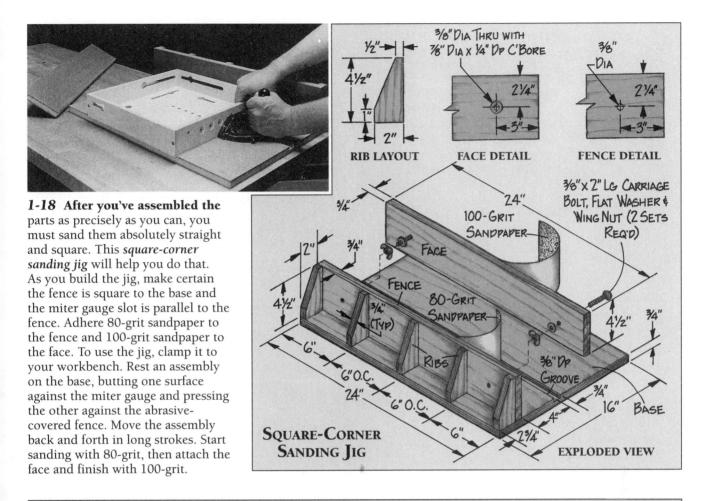

1-18 After you've assembled the parts as precisely as you can, you must sand them absolutely straight and square. This *square-corner sanding jig* will help you do that. As you build the jig, make certain the fence is square to the base and the miter gauge slot is parallel to the fence. Adhere 80-grit sandpaper to the fence and 100-grit sandpaper to the face. To use the jig, clamp it to your workbench. Rest an assembly on the base, butting one surface against the miter gauge and pressing the other against the abrasive-covered fence. Move the assembly back and forth in long strokes. Start sanding with 80-grit, then attach the face and finish with 100-grit.

HOLES, COUNTERBORES, AND SLOTS

Although the joinery for a shop-made accessory may be very simple, the machining often seems complex. Jigs and fixtures may require counterbored holes for hardware, pivot holes, slots for hardware to slide back and forth, and other special features. The apparent complexity is an illusion created by the number of special holes and slots needed. When considered individually, each of these features is simple to make.

Counterbored hole. To make a hole with a counterbore, clamp the wood to the drill press table. Drill the counterbore first, then change bits and drill the hole *without* changing the position of the wood. This will ensure that the hole is centered in the counterbore. **Note:** A counterbore is just a stopped hole, large enough to accept the head of the fastener and deep enough that the head will rest below the surface.

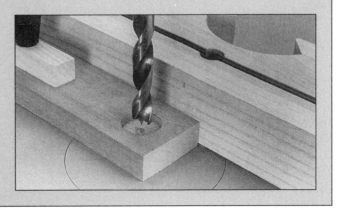

(continued) ▷

HOLES, COUNTERBORES, AND SLOTS — CONTINUED

Bushed pivot holes. When a pivot will see a lot of use, install a bushing in the pivot hole to keep the wood from wearing away. Drill the hole to the *outside* diameter of the bushing, and press the bushing in place. If the bushing seems loose in the hole, hold it in place with a cyanoacrylate glue such as Super Glue.

Fitted counterbore. Most counterbores are slightly larger than the head of the fastener. However, now and again you must fit a counterbore to the head of a hex bolt so it won't turn. To do this, make the counterbore the same diameter as the distance from flat to flat on the hex head. Then press the bolt head into the counterbore, or use a hex nut to help draw it in.

Straight slots. To cut a slot or a groove in a jig, use a router and a straight bit. Make the cut in several passes, routing just 1/16 inch deeper with each pass. By taking very small bites with each pass, you'll get a much more accurate cut. **Note:** For easy assembly, bore an *access hole* somewhere along the slot, slightly larger in diameter than the heads of the fasteners you wish to use in the slot. This turns an ordinary slot into a *keyhole slot* and lets you insert the hardware in it without having to disassemble the nuts and washers from the bolts. Drill the access hole *before* you rout the slot.

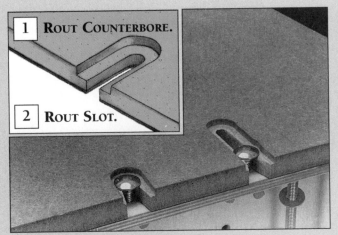

1 ROUT COUNTERBORE.

2 ROUT SLOT.

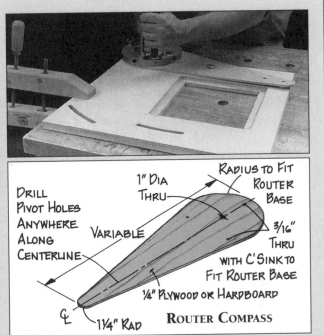

Router Compass

DRILL PIVOT HOLES ANYWHERE ALONG CENTERLINE

1" DIA THRU

VARIABLE

RADIUS TO FIT ROUTER BASE

3/16" THRU WITH C'SINK TO FIT ROUTER BASE

1/4" PLYWOOD OR HARDBOARD

CL

1¼" RAD

Counterbored slots. Occasionally, you must make a counterbored slot in a jig so the heads of the fasteners that slide in the slot will rest below the surface. Make this in much the same way that you would a counterbored hole — cut the counterbore first, then the slot. Position your router table fence or router guide to rout the slot. Select a straight bit a little larger than the heads of the fasteners and rout a groove deep enough to hold the heads. Without changing the position of the fence or the guide, mount a smaller straight bit in the router and cut a narrow slot in the center of the groove. The wider groove will form the counterbore.

Curved slots. On some jigs, the hardware must travel in an arc, sliding in a curved slot. To cut a curved slot, make a simple router compass and attach it to the base of the router. Lay out the slot on the jig, marking both the arc and its center. Use the compass as a guide when you cut the slot, pivoting the router and the straight bit around the center of the arc.

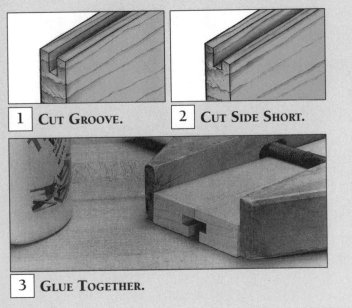

1 CUT GROOVE.

2 CUT SIDE SHORT.

3 GLUE TOGETHER.

T-slots. The traditional method for cutting T-slots is to use a router and a T-slot cutter. However, these cutters are available in limited sizes that will accommodate only flange bolts, closet bolts, and small hardware. To make a T-slot to fit a large carriage bolt or hex bolt, cut grooves in the edges of two separate boards, then cut one side of each groove short. Glue the two boards edge to edge to form a T-slot, as shown.

2

SAFETY AND
DUST COLLECTION

There's no denying that power tools are dangerous. Get too close to a spinning blade or bit, and it can cut you. Even if you're careful to maintain your distance, the blade or bit may grab the wood and throw it at you. Other moving parts, such as pulleys and belts, can pinch you and do a good deal of damage in short order. Even the sawdust generated by power tool woodworking is a hazard, causing health problems and ruining your machinery. Fortunately, there are several simple accessories that you can make to keep yourself clear of danger zones and reduce the sawdust to a minimum.

KEEPING OUT OF DANGER

A *danger zone* surrounds every running blade, cutter, and bit — once inside this zone, you cannot react in time to prevent injury when something goes wrong. Several types of jigs are designed specifically to keep you outside the danger zones and provide better control over the work.

FEEDING THE WORK

The most common are *pushers* — jigs that extend your reach so you can safely push boards past blades and cutters. A *push stick* has a notched end to catch the end or edge of a board. (*SEE FIGURE 2-1.*) A *push block* has a flat surface to hold a board flat on a table. A *push shoe* is similar to a push block, but it has a "heel" at one end to catch the edge of the board. (*SEE FIGURE 2-2.*) Also refer to the "Pusher" on page 63.

For many operations, you can't simply push the workpiece past the cutter — you must *hold* it as you do so. This is especially common when working with small workpieces. For these procedures, you must make a *handler* or *carriage* to hold and guide the workpiece. (*SEE FIGURE 2-3.*) Many special-purpose jigs are carriages that hold the wood in a specific relationship to the cutter. A tenoning jig, for example, holds a board vertical to a table saw blade. A tapering jig holds it at an angle.

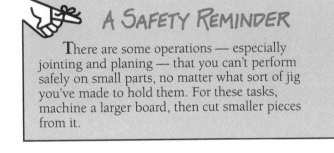

A SAFETY REMINDER

There are some operations — especially jointing and planing — that you can't perform safely on small parts, no matter what sort of jig you've made to hold them. For these tasks, machine a larger board, then cut smaller pieces from it.

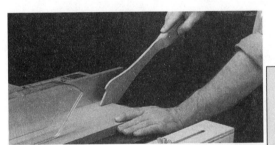

2-1 This *reversible push stick* has a thinned-out shaft to let you reach between a blade and a fence when maneuvering narrow stock. Because the design is reversible, you can use it with the bulge of the handle facing right or left — whichever keeps your hand farthest from the danger zone.

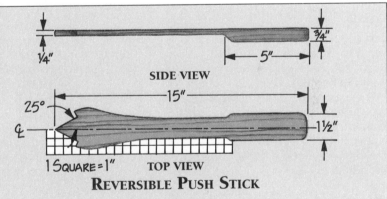

SIDE VIEW

¼"   ¾"   5"

25°   15"   1½"

1 SQUARE=1"   **TOP VIEW**

REVERSIBLE PUSH STICK

2-2 The *push shoe* shown has a movable heel that slides up out of the way when you don't need it. This lets you use the jig as both a push shoe and a push block.

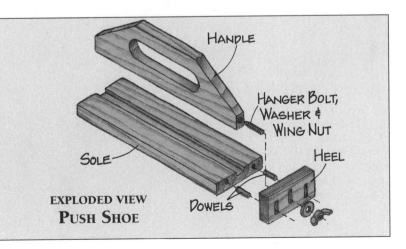

HANDLE

HANGER BOLT, WASHER & WING NUT

HEEL

SOLE

DOWELS

EXPLODED VIEW
PUSH SHOE

For help in guiding a workpiece or for protection against kickback, you can use *featherboards* (also called fingerboards and spring boards). These jigs have long, flexible fingers that hold the work against a table or a fence. Secure the featherboard to the tool, angling the fingers in the direction you wish to feed the wood. The wood slides forward smoothly, but the fingers prevent it from moving back. (*SEE FIGURES 2-4 AND 2-5.*)

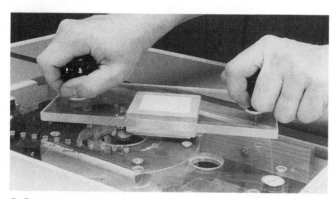

2-3 This *small-parts handler* is designed to help rout or shape small pieces. It's made from clear acrylic plastic so you can see the part as you rout it. Fasten the part to the bottom of the acrylic plate with double-faced carpet tape. Or, if you rout a lot of small parts, use a vacuum hold-down. (Refer to "Clamps" on page 48 for more information on vacuum clamping.) **Note:** When using carpet tape to hold a small part to the handler, clamp the two together for a few moments — the momentary pressure increases the strength of the adhesive bond.

2-4 *Featherboards* help guide the work and prevent it from kicking back. To make a featherboard, miter or round the end of a board with clear, straight grain. Cut several ⅛-inch-wide kerfs in this end, each several inches long, making ⅛-inch-wide fingers. Secure the featherboard to the tool vertically to hold the work down on a table and/or horizontally to hold it against a fence.

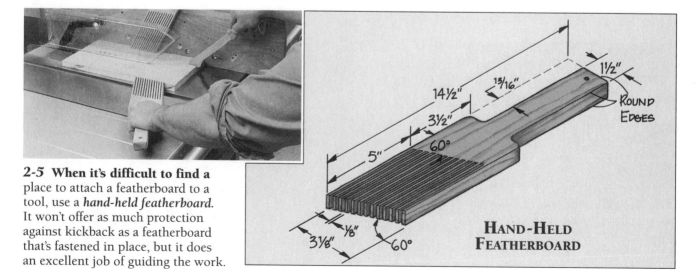

2-5 When it's difficult to find a place to attach a featherboard to a tool, use a *hand-held featherboard.* It won't offer as much protection against kickback as a featherboard that's fastened in place, but it does an excellent job of guiding the work.

HAND-HELD FEATHERBOARD

14½"
13/16"
1½"
ROUND EDGES
3½"
5"
60°
⅛"
3⅛"
60°

GUARDING THE CUTTER

Whenever a part of the blade is exposed, it makes good sense to cover it with a *guard*, provided the guard does not interfere with woodworking operations. (*SEE FIGURE 2-6.*) You also need to cover "pinch points" — places where your fingers might get caught between moving parts. (*SEE FIGURE 2-7.*) In some cases, you can make a guard do double duty as a measuring device or hold-down. (*SEE FIGURE 2-8.*)

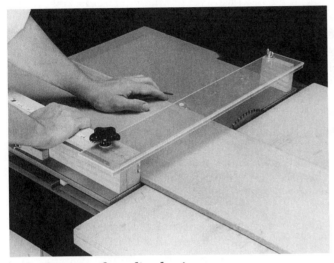

2-6 The strip of acrylic plastic on this sliding saw table serves as a guard to keep your fingers away from the saw blade and a shield to prevent the blade from pitching wood chips at you. You can use colored plastic to provide a visual reminder of where the danger zone begins and ends. The strip is carefully designed not to interfere with cutting operations, and its transparency lets you see the cut as it progresses. Refer to the "Sliding Cutoff Table" on page 89.

2-7 These odd-shaped plywood boxes cover the pulleys and belts on a shopmade speed changer for this band saw. Belts and pulleys are *pinch points* — danger zones created by moving parts that don't have sharp edges. Your hand, if it were to catch on a moving belt, would quickly be pulled between the belt and a pulley, amputating a finger or breaking a wrist. Other examples of pinch points include parts that come together in a scissors action (such as a collapsible frame) or rotary motion (meshing gears). All of these should be guarded.

2-8 Both of these guards do double duty; that is, they perform additional functions besides keeping you out of the danger zone. The jointer *feather-board guard* (left) helps hold the wood flat against the fence, while making it almost impossible for you to reach the cutterhead. The router table *depth gauge/guard* (right) detaches from the fence to measure the depth of cut. Refer to the "Lift-Top Router Table" on page 98.

CONTROLLING DUST

In one sense, your entire shop is a danger zone. The sawdust generated by your power tools creates an unhealthy environment. Even if you wear a dust mask, you will touch, ingest, and breathe in wood dust. This can irritate your skin, eyes, nose, and lungs. Constant exposure may contribute to severe allergies and respiratory problems such as emphysema. Additionally, sawdust can be unhealthy for your tools — fine dust will ruin bearings, bushings, switches, and electrical contacts. The most effective way to reduce these dangers is to collect the dust at its source, as you work, with shopmade dust pickups.

DESIGNING A DUST PICKUP

To create a dust pickup for a power tool, you must have a dust collector, not just a shop vacuum. (Refer to "Selecting a Dust Collector" on page 26.) Then decide on the likely *collection points*. Where will you hook the hose of the dust collector to the tool? The best collection point is usually as close to the blade or bit as possible, where the wood is first cut. Watch the cutting action of the tool carefully and note which way the cutter flings the sawdust. A band saw, for example, directs it down under the table, while a router table sends it toward the fence. Consequently, the best collection point for a band saw is under the table, near the blade; on a router table, it's behind the fence, near the bit. (*SEE FIGURES 2-9 THROUGH 2-12.*)

The size of the opening through which you collect the sawdust is extremely important. If the opening is too large, the dust collector won't be able to move the air fast enough to carry away the sawdust. But if you make it too small, the collector won't be able to draw in enough air.

Your dust collector moves a constant *volume* of air, measured in cubic feet per minute, or CFM. (You can find the CFM rating on the manufacturer's label.) The smaller the opening, the higher the air *velocity* needed to keep up with this volume. And high velocity is just what you need — the air must flow at least 3,500 feet per minute (FPM) to move the sawdust with it. Use this simple equation to determine the largest useful opening for your collector:

$$(\text{CFM} \div 3{,}500 \text{ FPM}) \times 144 = \text{Area}$$
$$(\text{in square inches})$$

For example, if your collector is rated at 400 CFM, then the largest opening you should use for a dust pickup is about 16½ square inches: (400 ÷ 3,500) × 144 = 16.46. This is roughly equal to the area of a hole 4½ inches in diameter. If the opening is any larger than that, the air velocity won't be high enough to pull the sawdust into the opening.

Furthermore, this consideration applies to the enclosed path (called a *run*) through which the sawdust travels. The cross section of the run at any one point must be no greater than the largest useful opening. If the air is drawn through a wide chamber (such as a box), the velocity will drop inside the chamber and the dust will settle out, possibly clogging the collector. To create a narrow run through a wide chamber, you must install airtight baffles that enclose the path inside the larger space. (*SEE FIGURE 2-13.*)

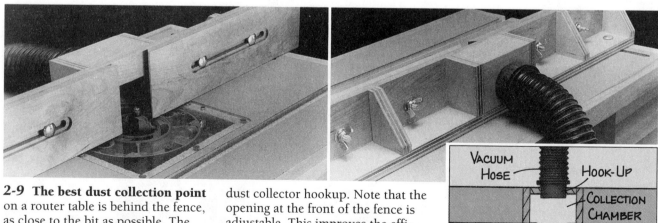

2-9 The best dust collection point on a router table is behind the fence, as close to the bit as possible. The small box-shaped chamber on the back of this fence helps catch wood chips and funnel them toward the dust collector hookup. Note that the opening at the front of the fence is adjustable. This improves the efficiency of the dust pickup — as the opening gets smaller, the air velocity increases and more dust is collected.

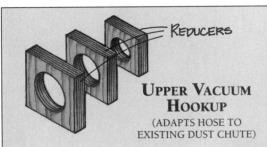

UPPER VACUUM HOOKUP
(ADAPTS HOSE TO EXISTING DUST CHUTE)

2-10 This band saw sports two dust pickups. This first collection point is just below the table, right as the blade leaves the lower guides. The second is at the bottom of the lower housing. The first pickup gets most of the fine dust, while the second captures the larger chips that settle to the bottom of the tool.

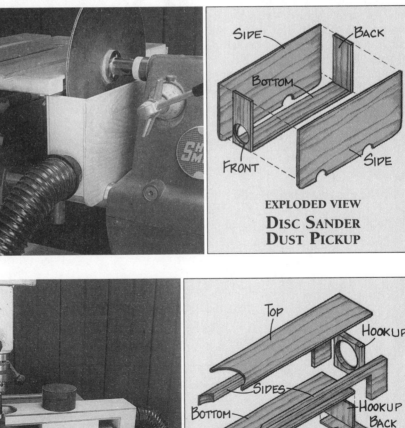

LOWER VACUUM HOOKUP
(ATTACHES HOSE TO TOOL HOUSING)

2-11 This disc sander dust pickup encases the lower half of the disc — the portion beneath the work surface. Since you sand on the part of the disc that rotates down, the abrasive flings the dust down into the pickup.

EXPLODED VIEW
DISC SANDER DUST PICKUP

2-12 A drill press doesn't create fine sawdust nor does it fling it everywhere. Consequently, you don't often need to collect the sawdust as you work. Most craftsmen simply brush off the machine when they've finished drilling. There are, however, occasions when you need to clear the chips as you make them. The drill press dust pickup will do the job. Weigh the jig down on the drill press table, positioning it so the opening partially surrounds the bit.

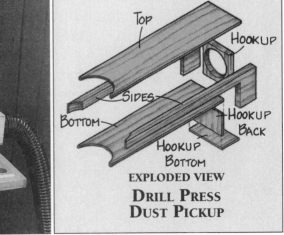

EXPLODED VIEW
DRILL PRESS DUST PICKUP

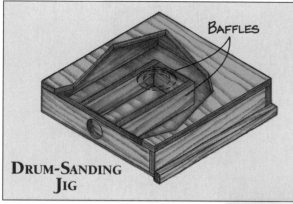

BAFFLES

DRUM-SANDING JIG

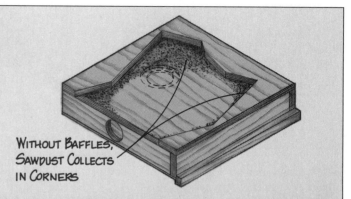

WITHOUT BAFFLES, SAWDUST COLLECTS IN CORNERS

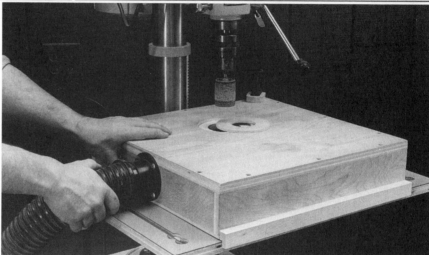

2-13 This *drum-sanding jig* has a vacuum hookup to collect the dust as you work. Note, however, that it's not just a hollow box. Inside the box are baffles to create a narrow run. These restrict the path of the air stream and keep the velocity high. If there were no baffles, the air velocity would drop inside the box and the corners would fill up with dust. **Note:** The baffles must completely enclose the run, making it reasonably airtight. If there are leaks, the efficiency of the dust collector will suffer.

By the same token, you shouldn't make the run or the opening too small or the air velocity too high. Your dust collector has limits — it can move only so much air with so much force. As the size of the pickup opening decreases or the run narrows, it reaches a point where the collector just can't pull the air through the pathway fast enough to keep up with the necessary volume, and the efficiency of the dust collector declines. You may have noticed this phenomenon if you've ever hooked a 1¼-inch shop vacuum hose to a dust collector that ordinarily uses 2½-inch hoses — the small hose will not pick up as much dust as the large one. A good rule of thumb is to size the openings of your dust pickups to pull air between 4,000 and 6,000 FPM.

What if the tool flings the sawdust over a wide area, or it's built in such a way that you can't possibly make a collector with a small opening? When this is the case, build a scoop or a funnel to collect the wood chips, positioning it so the sawdust settles in the narrow end. Install a vacuum hookup at the narrowest point. (*SEE FIGURES 2-14 THROUGH 2-16.*)

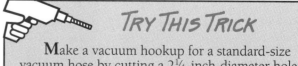

FOR YOUR INFORMATION

The force with which a dust collector moves the air is called *static pressure,* and it's measured by the number of inches the machine can pull a column of water up a tube of a given diameter. Although it becomes important when building a large dust collection system, static pressure is not a concern when making individual pickups.

TRY THIS TRICK

Make a vacuum hookup for a standard-size vacuum hose by cutting a 2¼-inch-diameter hole in a wooden part with a hole saw. This works just as well as a commercial flange hookup.

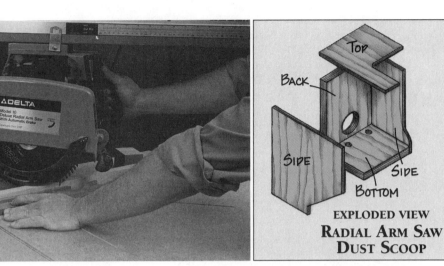

EXPLODED VIEW
RADIAL ARM SAW
DUST SCOOP

2-14 As it cuts, the radial arm saw flings most of the sawdust back into this box-shaped scoop. It hits the back of the scoop and settles to the bottom, near the pickup opening. The pickup whisks the dust away as it settles.

2-15 This jointer has a dust pickup built into the stand. The whirling knives throw the wood chips down, out the bottom of the machine. They enter a dust chute and drop down toward the pickup opening, where they are evacuated. The pickup opening is in a larger door that covers the lower end of the chute. This is because the jointer sometimes produces extremely large shavings that can clog the pickup. When this happens, simply open the door and clean out the chute.

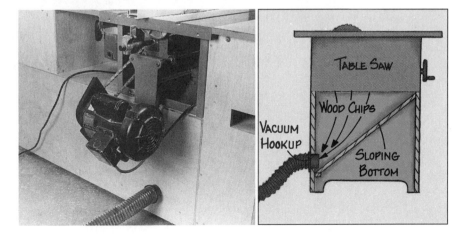

2-16 The dust collector on this table saw depends on gravity as much as vacuum to work. The wood chips settle on the sloping bottom of the cabinet and are funneled to the vacuum hookup at the back.

SELECTING A DUST COLLECTOR

When choosing a dust collector for your shop, pay careful attention to the CFM ratings. Because power tools produce a high volume of sawdust, they require a high-volume vacuum to collect that waste efficiently. Most home workshop tools need a collector that moves at least 350 CFM. Some especially "dirty" tools, like the planer and the band saw, require 400 CFM or more.

Don't expect an ordinary shop vacuum to make an efficient dust collector. Shop vacs are designed to move a low volume of air with a high amount of force — their CFM rating is usually under 150. They are very handy for cleaning up, but they won't move enough air to collect sawdust through a pickup.

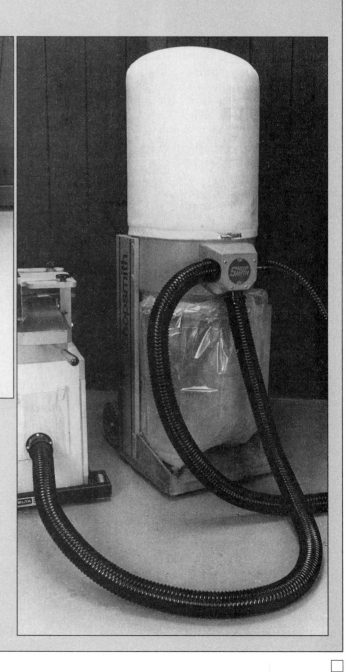

Although they share a superficial similarity — they both suck air through hoses — a *shop vacuum* (left) and a *dust collector* (right) are two different machines. Shop vacuums draw a low volume or air with an extremely high force, and are designed to clean up both wet and dry messes. They will pick up dirt, dust, and spilled liquids. Dust collectors generate less force, but they move a much larger volume of air. They will not pick up liquids, but they can evacuate sawdust from most woodworking tools just as fast as you can make it.

3

SUPPORT AND GUIDANCE

Whenever you cut, drill, or sand a workpiece, you must *support* it — hold it steady against the action of the power tool. Additionally, you must *guide* the workpiece (or the tool) in a straight line, an arc, or a precise pattern as you work. For example, the work surface on a table saw supports the work, while the fence guides it.

You can also build jigs and fixtures for support and guidance. Like a table saw, a shop-made router table has a supporting surface and a guiding fence. A compass jig supports the router and guides it in a circle, allowing you to cut arcs. A mortising template supports and guides a router in a pattern, routing a mortise. The challenge in building these accessories is to keep them *true*. Work surfaces must be flat, fences must be straight, compasses must describe a fair arc, and patterns must be precise.

SUPPORT: TABLES AND WORK SURFACES

When building a table or work surface, consider the load you will put on the surface and how much you will use it. The surface must be strong enough to support the weight of the workpiece and the force applied to it. It must also be durable enough to withstand normal wear and tear.

SURFACE MATERIALS

Medium-density fiberboard (MDF) and particleboard are usually the best materials for a supporting surface because they are stable and remain flat. Unfortunately, they aren't extremely strong or durable. Depending on your application, you may have to brace them to provide extra strength or cover them with a harder material to make them long wearing.

When you need extra strength or durability, use European birch plywood instead. It's not as stable as fiberboard and particleboard, but it remains fairly flat through the seasons. Avoid ordinary plywood and solid wood except when making jigs for one-time use — these are prone to warping and cupping.

MAKING A FLAT SURFACE

There are several methods for building a flat surface and keeping it that way.

BRACED SURFACE

One of the easiest methods is to make a simple frame to brace the surface material. The frame may be a simple rectangle (*ring*), several rectangles inside one another (*concentric rings*), or a rectangle with additional cross members (*ladder*). Make the frame from solid wood, attaching the frame members so the wood grain is parallel to the table surface. Since wood is stable along the grain, the frame won't stress the surface it braces. (*SEE FIGURES 3-1 AND 3-2.*)

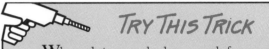

TRY THIS TRICK

When gluing up the bracework for a worktable, clamp the frame members to a perfectly flat surface (such as a saw table) while the glue dries. This will ensure that the assembled bracework is as flat as possible.

TORSION BOX

If you attach a second surface under a braced surface, sandwiching the framework between two "skins," you create a torsion box. This is an extremely rigid construction — the double skins distribute the load over the entire frame, keeping the structure flat. (*SEE FIGURE 3-3.*)

LAMINATED SHEET

If you need a thick, massive surface to absorb vibrations or withstand heavy blows, glue two or more pieces of MDF or particleboard face to face to make up the required thickness. Use the same material for

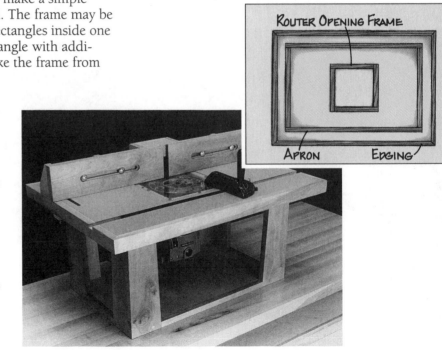

3-1 The MDF work surface on this router table is braced with three rectangular hardwood frames, each frame a different size and arranged one inside the other, as shown in the drawing. The largest frame is the hardwood edging around the perimeter of the table. The next largest forms the apron that attaches the work surface to the supporting legs. The smallest frame surrounds the opening where the router is mounted.

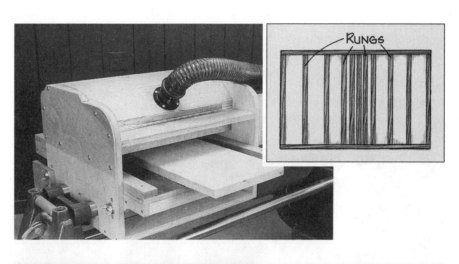

3-2 The work surface on this shop-made *thickness sander* is braced with a ladderlike frame. Note that the "rungs" on this ladder — the frame's cross members — are much closer together near the middle of the work surface, under the sanding drum. This arrangement helps provide additional support where the load is greatest.

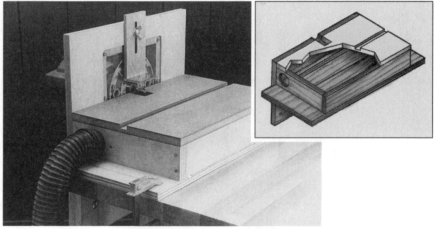

3-3 The base of this horizontal routing jig is a torsion box. The MDF work surface and the plywood bottom are the upper and lower skins, while the sides and ribs serve as the framework. This keeps the surface flat, despite the stress generated by a powerful router mounted to one side. **Note:** One additional advantage of a torsion box is that it is hollow and can be adapted to collect sawdust. The ribs serve as baffles to restrict and direct the air stream.

each layer so the laminated sheet expands and contracts uniformly. If you mix different materials, the assembly may warp.

SINGLE SHEET

The supporting surfaces on some jigs, such as sliding tables and cutoff boxes, must be as thin as possible. Make these from hardboard, MDF, particleboard, or, if strength is a concern, European birch plywood. Usually, you don't need to worry about strength — these work surfaces are supported by whatever tool they rest on. (*See Figure 3-4.*)

To increase the durability of a surface or reduce the friction when you slide boards across it, cover it with plastic laminate. To keep a laminate-covered work surface perfectly flat, apply plastic laminate to *both* faces. Or, coat the uncovered face with enamel paint or polyurethane. That way, both faces will absorb and release moisture at the same rate. If you leave one face uncovered and untreated, it will expand and contract faster than the covered face, and the work surface will cup.

3-4 The work surface on this *pipe clamp rack* is a single sheet of ¾-inch-thick particleboard. Although it sometimes holds an enormous amount of weight, it's sufficiently supported by a workbench and remains flat throughout the gluing operation. The scalloped racks along the front and back edges of the work surface also help to keep it flat.

You can also use tempered hardboard as a durable covering, although it's neither as hard nor as slick as laminate. However, it's less expensive and easy to apply. Simply tack it down with small brads and set the heads below the surface. When the hardboard covering wears out, pry it up and apply another.

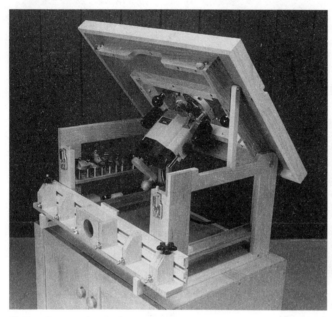

3-5 The work surface on this *lift-top router table* tilts to allow easy access to the router. The aprons are attached to the back legs with carriage bolts and stop nuts that serve as pivots. The surface has just two positions — down (horizontal) and up (raised 50 degrees from horizontal). It's supported in the up position by a simple hardwood brace that rests in a notch in the frame, as shown. The brace folds against the underside of the work surface when the table is down. Refer to the "Lift-Top Router Table" on page 98.

3-7 The tool rest on this shop- made flat grinder is attached to trunnions. The trunnions pivot on a fixed base, tilting 65 degrees. The rest can be secured at any angle in that range by locking the trunnions against the base. The slot in each trunnion is curved — a 65-degree segment of a circle — and the center of that circle is the pivot.

MAKING TILTING, SLIDING, AND ROLLING SURFACES

For some woodworking operations, you must tilt the work surface to adjust the angle of the work in relation to the tool. To make a surface tilt, attach it to a fixed base with a hinge or a pivot so it will move through a range of angles. Secure the surface at the desired angles with braces, slides, or trunnions. (*SEE FIGURES 3-5 THROUGH 3-7.*)

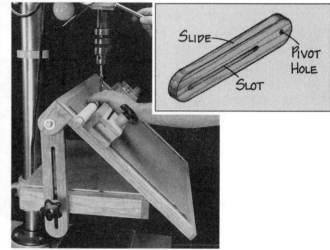

3-6 This *auxiliary drill press table* is attached to a fixed base with a piano hinge and tilts 55 degrees from horizontal. You can secure it at any tilt angle within this range by locking the slides against the base. Each slide has a pivot hole in one end and a long slot along its length. The pivoting end is attached to the tilting table, and the slot fits over a carriage bolt in the base. Refer to the "Tilting Drill Press Table" on page 111.

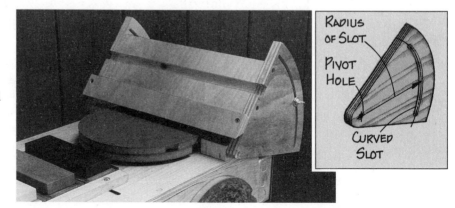

Other operations require a sliding or a rolling surface to help feed the work past a cutter or a bit. Sliding surfaces usually need to be guided so they travel in a straight line. You can use a fence or a straightedge to guide a sliding surface, or attach rails to the bottom that fit the miter gauge slots on your tool. (SEE FIGURE 3-8.) A rolling surface is stationary; it needs no guidance. Instead, you must secure rollers or bearings at the proper height to guide the wood. (SEE FIGURE 3-9.)

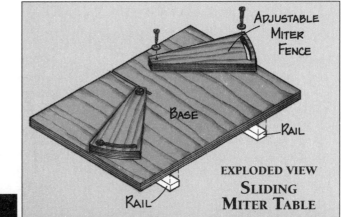

EXPLODED VIEW
SLIDING MITER TABLE

3-8 This *sliding miter table* glides back and forth across the saw table, guided by rails. The rails are cut to fit the miter gauge slots in the saw table as closely as possible. You can purchase steel miter gauge rails from several mail-order woodworking suppliers, or you can make your own. When making rails to fit a slot, use a wear-resistant material that will not expand or contract. One of the best choices is ultrahigh–molecular weight (UHMW) plastic. In addition to being extremely durable and stable, this material is very slick, reducing friction so that the jig slides easier.

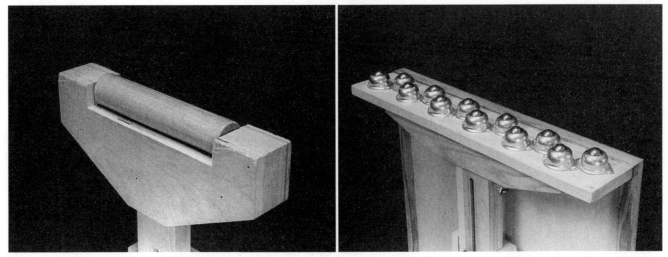

3-9 *Auxiliary support stands* extend the work surface of a power tool, making it easier for you to work with extra-long or extra-large stock. These stands often have rolling surfaces to support the work as you feed it over them. The stand on the left uses a rolling pin as a roller. This is inexpensive and effective, but it makes the stand uni-directional. That is, the roller must be aligned perpendicular to the direction in which you want the stock to feed. If it's off by a few degrees, it will pull the wood to the side. The stand on the right uses large metal ball bearings to provide a rolling surface. These are much more expensive, but they are omni-directional — they will feed the stock in any direction, no matter how the stand is situated.

GUIDANCE: FENCES AND STRAIGHTEDGES

DESIGNING A FENCE OR STRAIGHTEDGE

A fence guides the work or the tool along a face, while a straightedge guides it along an edge. In both cases, they must be dead straight. But there are other considerations as well. When designing a fence or a straightedge, ask yourself:

■ How long should the edge or the face be to provide adequate guidance? If it's too short, you'll have trouble guiding a long workpiece accurately.

■ Will you need to attach stops or featherboards? If so, you must cut slots or holes in the fence or straightedge, or provide some other means for attaching accessories.

■ Will you need to split the fence or make a cutout for a cutting tool? If so, you must add bracework that bridges the gap and reinforces the fence.

■ Will the sawdust interfere with the woodworking tasks you have to do with the fence or straightedge? If so, consider building a dust pickup into the fence.

FENCE AND STRAIGHTEDGE CONSTRUCTION

A fence or a straightedge must be strong enough along its length that it doesn't bow under normal pressure, and stable enough to remain straight over a long period of time. Both wood and plywood, or a mixture of the two, work well.

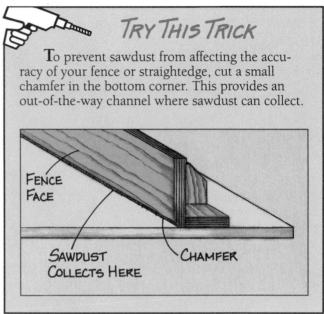

TRY THIS TRICK

To prevent sawdust from affecting the accuracy of your fence or straightedge, cut a small chamfer in the bottom corner. This provides an out-of-the-way channel where sawdust can collect.

FENCE FACE

SAWDUST COLLECTS HERE   CHAMFER

There are three basic designs for these fixtures. A typical straightedge is just a rectangular *bar* — a length of wood or plywood with straight edges. (*SEE FIGURE 3-10.*) A simple fence usually consists of a vertical face glued to a horizontal base to form an *L-beam.* (*SEE FIGURE 3-11.*) The base keeps the face from bowing when you hold the work against it. If you

STRAIGHTEDGE

EXPLODED VIEW
T-SQUARE
ROUTING GUIDE

CROSSBAR

3-10 A T-square routing guide consists of two rectangular bars — a straightedge and a crossbar — joined at right angles to one another. The straightedge guides the router, while the crossbar helps square the jig to the edge of the work.

need a stronger structure, add a top to make a *box*. (*See Figure 3-12.*)

You can cut out or split the guiding surface of any of these constructions to accommodate bits and cutters. (*See Figure 3-13.*) Additionally, you can make the halves of a split face *movable*, letting you adjust the opening between them or change their front-to-back positions independently. (*See Figure 3-14.*)

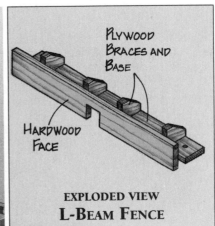

TRY THIS TRICK

To true a plywood straightedge, glue a ¼-inch-thick strip of hardwood to the edge and joint the strip. If you attempt to joint an uncovered plywood edge, the glue between the plies will tear up the jointer knives.

3-11 The fence on this router table is a simple L-beam with a cutout for the router bit. To make an *L-beam fence,* glue a hardwood face to a plywood base, and reinforce the assembly with braces every 6 to 8

inches to keep the face and base precisely 90 degrees to one another. After assembly, joint the hardwood face perfectly flat, straight, and square to the bottom. **Note:** If you assemble the parts of the fence with

screws or other metal fasteners, recess the heads well below the surface of the face so they won't nick the jointer knives.

EXPLODED VIEW
L-BEAM FENCE

3-12 This *reversible drill press fence* has two working surfaces — one side has a single long face, while the other has a split face and a cutout. The split side is useful for some routing, grinding, and drum-sanding operations. The top is slotted to attach stops and other accessories.

To build the fence, join the base, faces, and top to make a long box, adding interior bracework as you assemble the pieces to keep the parts square to one another. Make the faces from hardwood so you can true them on a jointer.

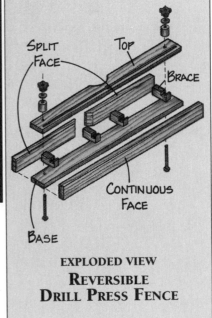

EXPLODED VIEW
REVERSIBLE
DRILL PRESS FENCE

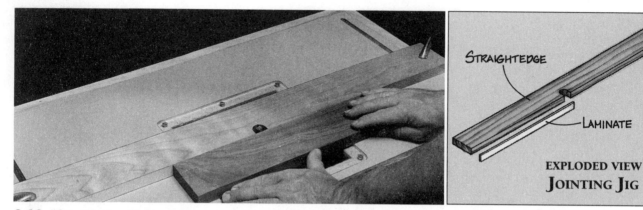

3-13 **This** *jointing jig* **lets you use** a router table to do edge jointing. Take a simple straightedge and saw a small cutout in the center of one edge, a little larger in diameter than a 1-inch straight bit. Apply a strip of plastic laminate to one half of the edge so the outfeed surface is offset slightly closer to the front of the router table than the infeed surface.

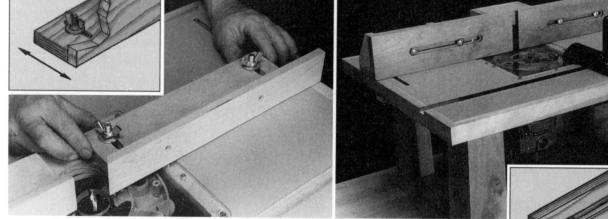

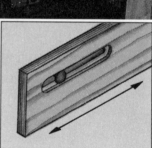

3-14 **Shown are two** *split fences,* each with movable faces, made for the same router table. On one, the face halves move front to back, allowing you to offset them from each other. On the other, the halves move side to side, letting you adjust the opening between them. In both cases, the moving parts are slotted to fit over carriage bolts.

GUIDES FOR CUTTING CURVES, CONTOURS, AND HOLES

Fences and straightedges work by guiding tools and workpieces in a straight line to make a straight cut. However, you can also devise jigs that will help you create precise curves, circles, holes, mortises, and patterns.

CUTTING CIRCLES AND CURVES

The trick to cutting a circle or a curve with a constant radius is to rotate the work or the power tool around a fixed *pivot*. The "Router Compass" on page 17 is a good example. This jig swings the router around a pivot, cutting all or part of a circle. An ordinary fastener — nail, screw, or bolt — serves as the pivot.

In the case of a router compass, the workpiece is fixed while the power tool moves. However, you can also make a jig that swings a workpiece in a circle or an arc past a band saw, scroll saw, or sander. (*See Figure 3-15.*) To do this, rotate the work around a pivot. Again, you can use a fastener as a pivot, or just the point of a nail or screw.

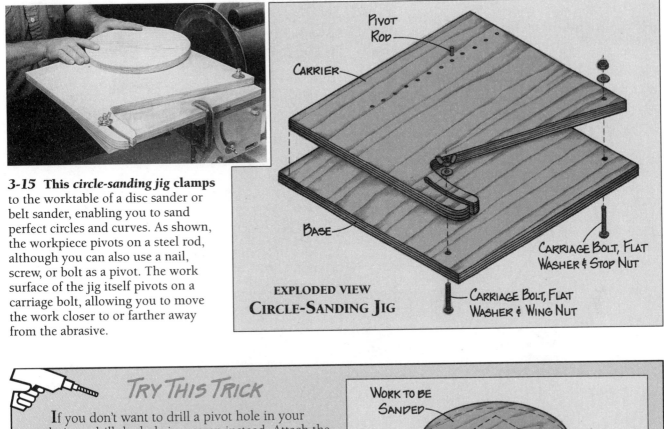

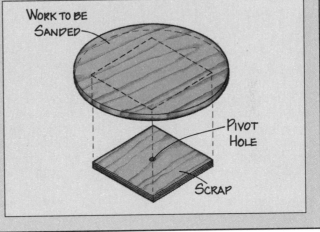

3-15 This *circle-sanding jig* clamps to the worktable of a disc sander or belt sander, enabling you to sand perfect circles and curves. As shown, the workpiece pivots on a steel rod, although you can also use a nail, screw, or bolt as a pivot. The work surface of the jig itself pivots on a carriage bolt, allowing you to move the work closer to or farther away from the abrasive.

EXPLODED VIEW
CIRCLE-SANDING JIG

TRY THIS TRICK

If you don't want to drill a pivot hole in your workpiece, drill the hole in a scrap instead. Attach the scrap to the work with double-faced carpet tape. Cut or sand the curve, rotating the work and the scrap. Detach the scrap from the work when you're finished.

CUTTING PATTERNS AND MORTISES

You can guide a router to follow almost any contour, routing both inside and outside shapes. Duplicate patterns, cut recesses for inlays, create odd-shaped slots for tambours, and make mortises, all by making a *template* for the router to follow. Cut templates from a stable material such as particleboard or MDF. Carefully sand or file the guiding edges so they are as smooth as possible — every little imperfection in the template will be duplicated in the routed shape. For maximum accuracy, cut your templates wide of the layout lines, then file or sand up to the lines.

There are two simple setups for pattern routing. Use a piloted bit, such as a *pattern-cutting bit* or a *flush-trim bit,* to follow the template. Or mount a *guide bushing* to the sole of your router so the bit protrudes through it. (*SEE FIGURE 3-16.*) Cut a template to the proper size and shape and attach it to the workpiece. Follow the template with the pilot bearing or the guide bushing, routing the shape you want. (*SEE FIGURES 3-17 AND 3-18.*)

3-16 Both a *pattern-cutting bit* and a *flush-trim bit* have pilot bearings that allow you to follow a template as you rout. The difference is that a pattern-cutting bit has a bearing at the top of the cutter, while a flush-trim bit has a bearing at the bottom. The bearings are precisely the same diameters as their bits, letting you cut a template to the exact size and shape you want to rout. You can also follow a template with a *guide bushing and straight bit*. However, the guide bushing is larger than the bit. Consequently, the template must be a slightly different size than the shape you wish to rout.

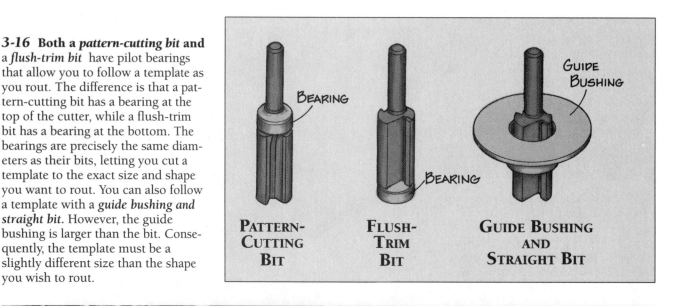

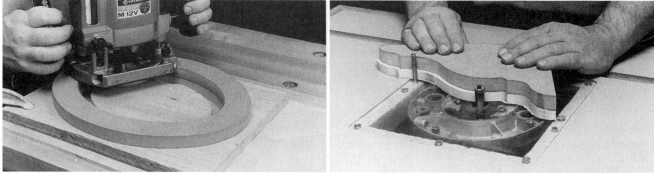

3-17 When using a *pattern-cutting bit* (left), cut the template the same size as the shape you want to rout and attach it to the *top* of the workpiece. When using a *flush-trim bit* (right), either attach the template to the *bottom* of the work or use the bit upside down in a router table, as shown. Both the oval frame template and the shelf bracket template are attached to their respective workpieces with double-faced carpet tape.

However, you can also use screws and nails as long as you're careful to place them where they won't be nicked by the router bit.

3-18 When routing a shape with a guide bushing and a straight bit, make the template a slightly different size than the shape you want to create. This compensates for the difference in diameters between the bushing and the bit. When cutting an *outside* shape, make the template *smaller;* for an *inside* shape, make it *larger.* The template shown is designed to rout mortises. Since these are inside shapes, the opening in the template is slightly larger than the completed mortise.

DRILLING HOLES

One of the easiest ways to drill holes where you want them is to make a *drill guide* and attach it to the workpiece. If you will use the guide just to bore a few holes, cut a block of hard, dense wood to fit over the workpiece and drill guide holes at the proper positions and angles in the block. (*See Figure 3-19.*) As you continue to use the drill guide, however, the bit will enlarge the guide holes and gradually reduce the jig's accuracy. To make a drill guide that can be used over and over again without losing accuracy, install hardened steel *guide bushings* in the guide's holes. (*See Figure 3-20.*)

3-19 This hardwood *drill guide* fits over the mitered corner of a box and guides a drill bit to bore dowel holes across the joint. The installed dowels strengthen the joint and add decoration. And this is just one application — you can fashion a drill guide to fit almost any assembly and to guide any size of bit. There are two drawbacks, however. First, you must use a bit that's the same diameter all along the length of its body, such as a twist bit or a brad-point bit. The jig won't work with spade bits, Forstner bits, and the like. Second, the action of the bit quickly wears away the wood, enlarging the hole. As you continue to use the jig, it becomes more and more inaccurate.

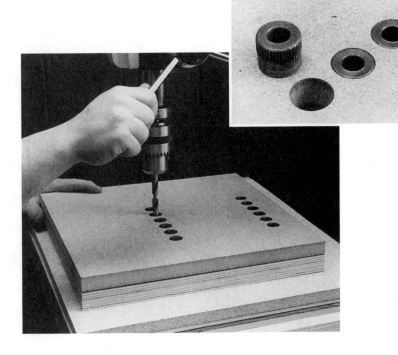

3-20 If you intend to use your drill guide over and over again, line the guide holes with hardened steel *guide bushings*. These prevent the bits from enlarging the holes. You can purchase these bushings from most mail-order woodworking supply houses. Unfortunately, they are commonly available in only a few sizes.

4

MEASURING AND POSITIONING

To do precision wood-working, you must lay out and measure the work, set up and adjust the tools, then position the work or the tools properly for each operation — all with unfailing accuracy. You can devise jigs and fixtures to help you perform each of these tasks. For example, a radial arm saw fence with a horizontal rule lets you measure the length of a board as you cut. A router table fence with a vertical scale makes it easier to adjust the height of the bit above the table surface. A miter gauge extension with an adjustable stop automatically positions the work when cutting duplicate lengths on a table saw.

These are not difficult jigs to design or make. Oftentimes, all you have to do is attach a rule, a scale, or a stop to a convenient surface.

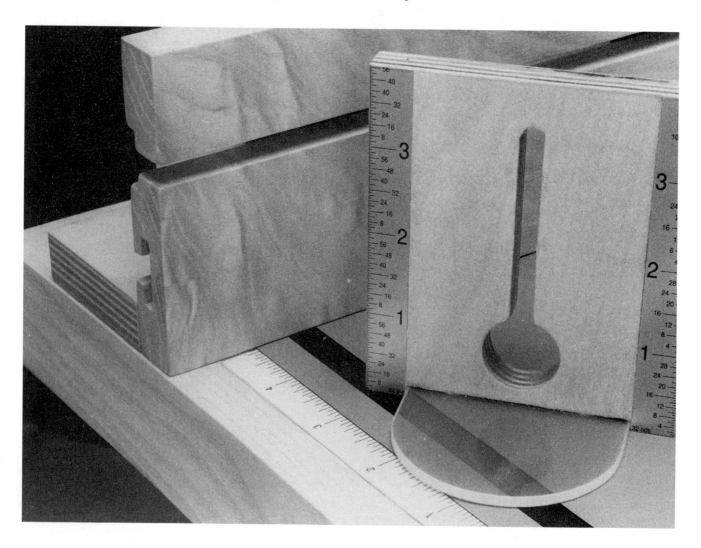

MEASUREMENT AND LAYOUT

LINEAR MEASURE

The type of measurement you make most often in woodworking is *linear measure,* as when measuring the length of a board or the height of a cutter above the table surface. The most common tool for linear measure is a rule or scale, and there are many rules designed specifically for use in jigs and fixtures. Most mail-order woodworking suppliers carry adhesive-backed rules that read left, right, or out from the center. (*See Figures 4-1 and 4-2.*)

A rule, however, isn't the only means of linear measure, nor is it the best for all operations. If you have to make the same measurements again and again, a *storystick* (a long, straight stick with marks along one edge) is more convenient. (*See Figure 4-3.*) When you must transfer measurements from one place to another, a *slide rule* (two sticks that slide parallel to one another) is handy. (*See Figure 4-4.*)

4-1 The fence on this sliding table has a rule that reads from right to left, letting you measure the boards as you cut them to length. The rule is installed in a shallow rabbet with its surface slightly below that of the fence face. (This helps keep the rule from wearing.) Also note that the rule reads upside down so that when you lean over the fence to read it, the numbers appear right side up.

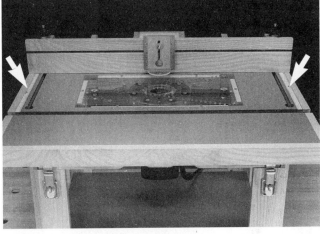

4-2 This router table has two centering scales on either side of the router. The "0" mark on each scale is aligned with the center of the router bit. By doing a little addition or subtraction, you can use these scales to position the fence precisely in relation to the bit.

4-3 A *storystick* is a rule that you make for one specific set of measurements. The storystick shown is being used to lay out a set of hinge mortises on a door and a door frame. This ensures that the positions of the mortises on each piece are identical.

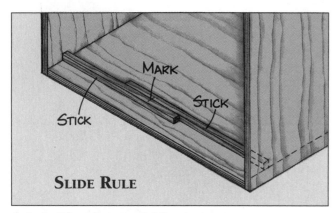

SLIDE RULE

4-4 A *slide rule* is useful for transferring measurements, particularly inside dimensions such as a door opening or the depth of a cabinet. Make this jig from any two straight sticks. Just hold the sticks parallel to one another and slide them in opposite directions until the ends butt against opposite surfaces. Make a mark across both sticks, remove them from the area, and lay them on a flat surface. Align the marks again and measure from end to end with a tape measure or rule.

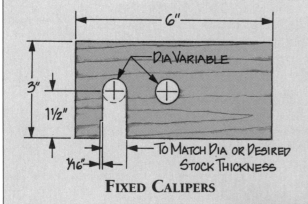

FIXED CALIPERS

4-5 You can make *fixed calipers* from a scrap of any stable material. Just cut a notch in the edge with an opening the same size as the dimension you want to measure. The calipers shown are designed to measure the diameter of a round tenon. The opening has a 1/16-inch step on one side. This tells you when the tenon is approaching the desired size. When you cut the tenon to the correct size, it slips past the step, all the way into the notch.

Gauging the thickness of a board or the diameter of a turning is another form of linear measure. Ordinarily, this is done with calipers, but if you frequently plane boards to the same thickness or turn to the same diameter, *fixed calipers* are quicker and easier to use. (*SEE FIGURE 4-5.*)

ANGULAR MEASURE

Measuring angles on a jig isn't quite as easy — there are no self-stick protractors available. Many craftsmen make their own by carefully marking degree lines on a surface of the jig. If you need more precision, you can incorporate a metal or plastic protractor into a jig. (*SEE FIGURE 4-6.*) Or, make wooden wedges to set often-used angles. (*SEE FIGURE 4-7.*)

MARKING AND LAYOUT

In addition to measuring inches and angles, you can design jigs to help mark stock and lay out work. An ordinary yardstick makes a great beam compass — just drill 1/8-inch-diameter holes at the inch marks, drive a nail through one hole to make a pivot, and insert the point of a pencil through another. You can also make a marking tool from a storystick. Drive small wire brads partway into the wood at the marks and clip off their heads about 1/8 inch above the wood surface. Use the protruding brads to scratch layout lines onto the workpiece.

And there are many other possibilities for marking tools. You can make jigs to help mark any surface, simple or complex, no matter what the geometry. *FIGURE 4-8* shows several additional shop-made marking tools.

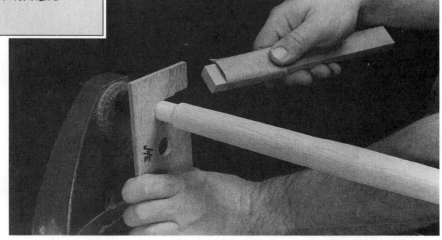

4-6 This *bevel-setting jig* measures the angle of the cutting edge when sharpening a chisel or a plane iron. A wooden post with a magnet mortised into its base supports a small plastic protractor. The indicator is a straight length of wire that pivots freely on the same bolt that holds the protractor to the post.

4-7 You can use a wooden *wedge* to help set the angle of this tilting drill press table. Just cut the wedge so one of the corners is the angle you need and insert the wedge between the tilting table and the fixed base. Adjust the table angle until it rests solidly on the wedge.

4-8 Here are several simple marking jigs, each designed for a specific marking or layout task. The *slope gauge* (1) helps you to mark lines 10 degrees off perpendicular, right or left, when laying out dovetail joints. The *V-shaped straightedge* (2) is made from two long, straight sticks, joined edge to face. This jig allows you to mark straight lines down the length of dowels and turned cylinders. A *center finder* (3) consists of three short sticks that are joined so the middle stick splits the angle between the two on the outside. When you slip the outside sticks over a round workpiece, the middle stick crosses its center. A *preacher* (4) is notched to fit over a aseboard molding and is used to mark the molding to the correct length so it will butt against the edge of a door casing. Set the molding in place, put the preacher over the molding, and hold the preacher against the casing. Then use the preacher as a guide to draw a straight line across the molding.

POSITIONING THE WORKPIECE

STOPS

When you need to either place a workpiece or a tool just so for an operation or halt the operation at a certain point, the all-purpose positioning jig is a *stop*. You can attach a stop to a fence or a straightedge to form a corner that cradles a rectangular board. Press the work against the fence and the stop to hold it in position on the power tool. For example, you can attach a stop to the fence of a radial arm saw to cut the work to a specific length. A stop on a drill press fence positions the work to drill a hole at a specific location. (*See Figure 4-9.*)

Or you can use the stop as a barrier. Feed the work or the tool along the straightedge until it reaches the stop — this arrests the operation. You can make a blind groove or dado in this manner. Attach a stop to the fence of a table saw to halt the board when the cut is the correct length. Or, clamp it to a router guide to stop a hand-held router. Use two stops to make a mortise — one to position the board when starting the mortise, and the second to arrest the cut when the mortise is the proper length. (*See Figure 4-10.*)

4-9 The *L-shaped stop* clamped to the fence of this drill press positions the work to drill a hole a specific distance away from the corner of a board. By flipping the boards end for end and face for face, you can drill holes in all four corners of each part. Each hole will be precisely the same distance away from the nearest end and edge.

EXPLODED VIEW
L-SHAPED STOP

4-10 This *mortising fence* is 48 inches long and has a slot running almost the entire length of the face. There are two stops mounted in this slot that you can position anywhere along the fence. To make a mortise, clamp the fence to a router table. Use one stop to position the work to start the mortise, and the other to halt the work when you've cut the mortise to the desired length. Hold the board so the end that you want to cut is slightly above the router bit, and place the other end against the first stop. Keeping the board against the fence, slowly lower it onto the bit and feed it toward the second stop.

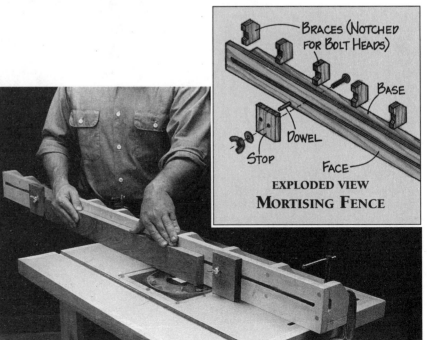

EXPLODED VIEW
MORTISING FENCE

You can make stops in different sizes and configurations, depending on your application. A stop can be just a single piece of wood or it can be more complex. (*SEE FIGURES 4-11 THROUGH 4-13.*) When designing a stop, consider:

■ What are the size and shape of the object you need to position? The surface of the stop may need to conform to a specific angle or contour.

■ Should you allow for sawdust buildup? If the operation is fairly "dirty," cut a dust channel or a chamfer in the stop.

■ Does the stop require fine adjustment for extremely precise positioning? To get the accuracy you need, incorporate an adjustment screw.

■ How will you secure the stop to the fence or the guide? There are many devices you can use — bolts, clamps, slots, and tracks — depending on your needs and preferences. Refer to "Construction Methods" on page 12 for more information on your options.

For some applications, you can make a stop just by cutting a notch or drilling a hole. If a jig includes two pieces of wood that slide together, and you often need to return these pieces to a certain position, drill holes through both boards when they are aligned. All you need to do to find that position again is line up the holes and insert a dowel pin through them. (*SEE FIGURE 4-14.*)

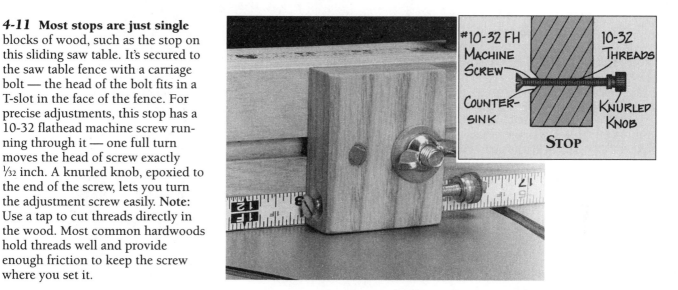

4-11 Most stops are just single blocks of wood, such as the stop on this sliding saw table. It's secured to the saw table fence with a carriage bolt — the head of the bolt fits in a T-slot in the face of the fence. For precise adjustments, this stop has a 10-32 flathead machine screw running through it — one full turn moves the head of screw exactly 1/32 inch. A knurled knob, epoxied to the end of the screw, lets you turn the adjustment screw easily. **Note:** Use a tap to cut threads directly in the wood. Most common hardwoods hold threads well and provide enough friction to keep the screw where you set it.

4-12 These *flip-up stops* are hinged so you can flip them up and out of the way. This lets you attach multiple stops to a fence or straightedge and use them to locate a workpiece in several different positions. In the setup shown, the stops are arranged to locate the same workpiece in two different positions on a drill press. Place the end of the board against the first stop to drill one hole, then flip the stop up and slide the board against the second stop to position it for the next hole.

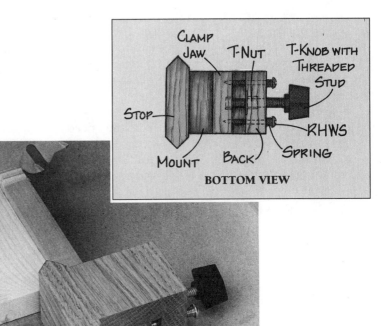

4-13 **The stop on this radial arm**
saw has a built-in clamp to hold it in
place. To secure the stop, just place it
over the fence and tighten the knob.
Note that the edges of the stop —
the surfaces that do the actual stop-
ping — are double-mitered and come
to points. The sawdust builds up
behind the points, where it is less
likely to interfere with the operation.

4-14 **Although this *support stand***
will adjust to any height between 27
and 45 inches, it's used almost exclusively at heights for a few specific
tools — a table saw, band saw, drill
press, router table, and jointer. There
is a single hole in the side and several
holes in the supporting post to serve
as stops. These help set the proper
height. To adjust the stand to the
height of the table saw, align the hole
in the side with the table saw hole on
the post, and insert a dowel through
both holes.

INCREMENTAL POSITIONING

Some woodworking operations require that you move and position the work in precise *increments*. When making a finger joint, for example, you must move the board a precise distance before cutting each finger. The distance the board moves — the increment — must be absolutely the same for each cut. There are several common methods for incremental positioning.

1 **This drill press setup uses** two *stops* — one fixed and one movable — to drill evenly spaced holes. Clamp the L-shaped stop to the drill press fence a specific distance from the chuck. Drill a hole in the work, insert the movable dowel stop in the hole, then slide the work to the left until the dowel butts against the L-shaped stop. Drill another hole, move the dowel to the new hole, and repeat. Each time you do this, the work will move the same distance to the left, and the holes will all be the same distance apart.

EXPLODED VIEW
FINGER JIG

STOP

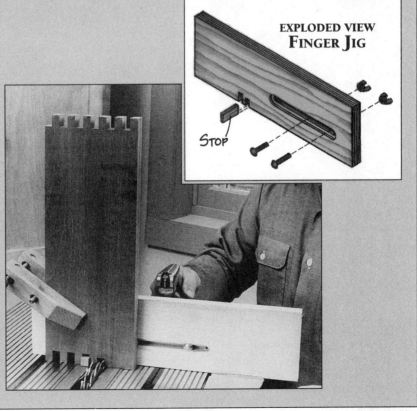

2 **This *finger jig* uses a stop** to position the wood before cutting each finger with a dado cutter. Set up the cutter to make a notch the same width as the stop. Attach the jig to a miter gauge and position it so the distance between the stop and the cutter is equal to the width of the stop. Butt the wood against the stop and cut a notch, creating a single finger. Shift the workpiece toward the stop, fitting the newly cut notch over the stop. Cut another notch and repeat as many times as necessary to make all the fingers. Each finger will be spaced precisely the same.

(continued) ▷

INCREMENTAL POSITIONING — CONTINUED

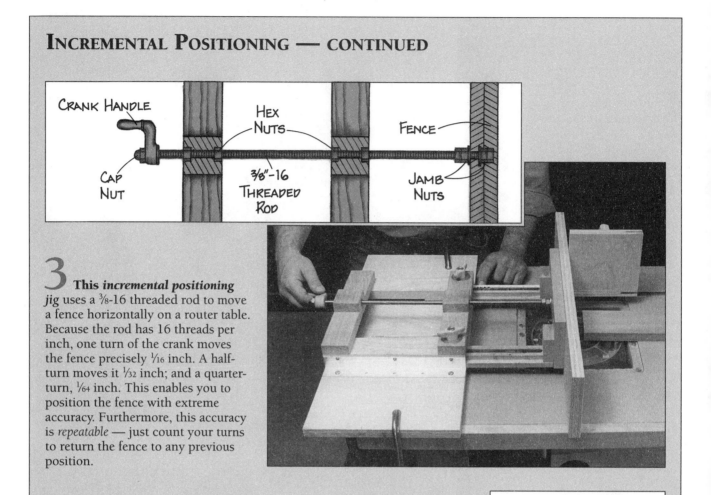

3 **This** *incremental positioning jig* uses a ⅜-16 threaded rod to move a fence horizontally on a router table. Because the rod has 16 threads per inch, one turn of the crank moves the fence precisely ¹⁄₁₆ inch. A half-turn moves it ¹⁄₃₂ inch; and a quarter-turn, ¹⁄₆₄ inch. This enables you to position the fence with extreme accuracy. Furthermore, this accuracy is *repeatable* — just count your turns to return the fence to any previous position.

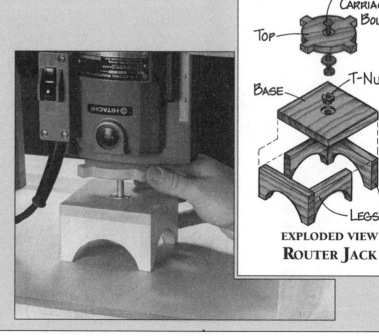

4 **Like the incremental posi**tioning jig, this *router jack* also uses threaded hardware for positioning. But unlike most positioning jigs, which move horizontally, this one moves vertically. A ⅜-16 carriage bolt and a T-nut drive the top of the jack up or down, which raises or lowers the router. Because the bolt has 16 threads per inch, one full turn moves the router ¹⁄₁₆ inch; one half-turn moves it ¹⁄₃₂ inch; and one quarter-turn, ¹⁄₆₄ inch. This lets you set the depth of cut precisely.

EXPLODED VIEW
ROUTER JACK

5

CLAMPING AND ASSEMBLING

There's a lot of truth to the old workshop joke, "If God had intended man to work wood, he would have given him three hands." Sometimes, when machining a workpiece, you cannot guide the wood or hold it in position with two hands alone — the oper-ation might take your fingers dangerously close to a cutter, or the workpiece might be too large or awkward to hold steady. You need a third hand — a clamp, a hold-down, or some other holding device to secure the work and make the operation safe.

You run into a similar problem when assembling a project — two hands are not enough. You need clamps or other holding fixtures to keep the parts together while the glue dries or as you install the fasteners.

CLAMPS

Some jigs are clamps — their sole purpose is to hold the wood in place during a woodworking operation. Others incorporate clamps in their design to fasten the wood to the jig. In both cases, the clamping device applies pressure to the work to secure it. There are several different ways to generate this pressure.

WEDGES

The simplest (and oldest) clamping device is a wedge. When you drive a wedge between two objects, it presses against both of them. You can use this pressure to secure a board in a jig or hold it steady on a workbench while you work on it. Build a frame that you can secure to the jig or the bench, place the work inside the frame, and drive wedges between the frame members and the work to clamp it in place. (*See Figure 5-1.*)

FOR BEST RESULTS

Cut the wedges with a gradual taper — 15 degrees or less. The shallower the slope on a wedge, the more securely it locks in place. Wedges with slopes that are too steep may come loose.

SCREWS

A screw is a wedge wound around a cylinder — the angled edge of the wedge becomes the threads on the screw. As you turn the screw, it rides along a set of matching threads inside a *nut*. Commercially made hand screws, C-clamps, and bar clamps all use screw devices to apply pressure. You can build your own clamps around threaded hardware such as carriage bolts, hex bolts, threaded rods, or wood screws. For example, a *violin clamp* — one of the simplest clamps you can make — consists of two disc-shaped jaws that fit over a bolt. The jaws are squeezed together by a nut. (*See Figure 5-2.*)

There are many variations on the screw clamp. You can apply pressure either by rotating the screw or by turning a nut or a knob that fits over it. (*See Figure 5-3.*) A *fulcrum* can extend the reach of a screw clamp to apply pressure several inches out from the shaft of the bolt. (*See Figure 5-4.*) *Springs* will automatically open the jaws when you loosen the clamp. (*See Figure 5-5.*) You can even use screws to press things apart rather than squeeze them together. (*See Figure 5-6.*)

5-1 A *planing jig* uses wedges to hold a board by its edges inside a simple frame. When the frame is clamped to your workbench, you can surface the board with a router and a large-diameter straight bit. This planing technique is time-consuming, but it's useful for surfacing figured wood that would chip or tear if sent through a planer. You can also use the jig to remove twists and cups from wide boards. The boards are secured in the frame with wedges. Notice the wedges are used in *pairs,* and the wedges in each pair are driven in opposite directions. This arrangement has several advantages over other types of clamps. The wedges lie flat, they are less likely to slip, and the pressure is more evenly distributed.

5-2 On the *violin clamp* (left), a single carriage bolt and wing nut squeeze two disc-shaped jaws together. The clamping pressure is greatest near the carriage bolt — it drops off as you get closer to the edge of the disc. The *honing guide* (right) incorporates a clamp that uses two carriage bolts and wing nuts. These draw a rectangular clamping bar down against a chisel to secure it in the guide. This arrangement helps to distribute the pressure evenly across the bar.

5-3 Although there are many designs for screw clamps, they all have a threaded *screw* and a *nut* to generate pressure. There are three ways to transfer this pressure and use it to hold the work. (1) Turn the nut to apply pressure. Often the nut is shaped so you can turn it easily, such as a wing nut or a star knob with a threaded insert. (2) Turn the screw so the *head* applies pressure. The head may be shaped to turn easily, such as a thumbscrew or a knob with a threaded stud. (3) Turn the screw so the *foot* applies pressure. The foot is sometimes connected to a clamp pad or a jaw.

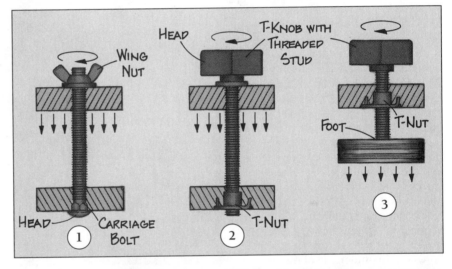

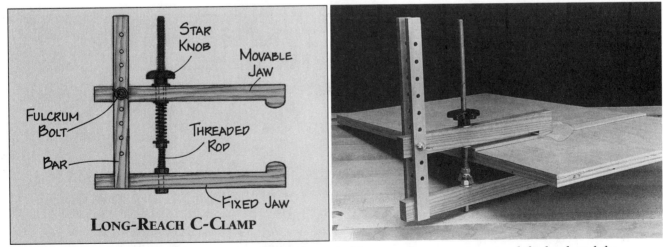

LONG-REACH C-CLAMP

5-4 This shop-made *long-reach* *C-clamp* uses a threaded rod and a star knob to generate the clamping pressure. As you turn the knob, the *movable jaw* pivots on a carriage bolt.

This bolt serves as a *fulcrum* and transfers the clamping pressure out to the end of the jaw. Without a fulcrum, most of the clamping pressure would be generated in the immediate area around the knob and the threaded rod. The pressure would grow weaker farther out along the jaw.

FOR YOUR INFORMATION

When building a clamp, the diameter of the screw has nothing to do with the amount of pressure it delivers — a large-diameter screw only makes the clamp sturdier. Should you need to apply more pressure, either increase the length or diameter of the handle used to turn the screw (or the nut), or use a screw with a finer thread pitch. Both changes will give you more leverage.

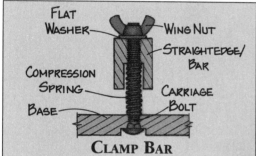

CLAMP BAR

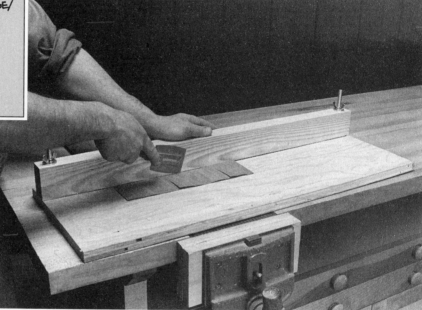

5-5 This *clamp bar* is both a clamp and a straightedge. The bar secures the work to its base and serves as a guide for a router or a saw. The bar is mounted to the base with carriage bolts and wing nuts. Between the bar and the base, there are compression springs that wind around the carriage bolts. These springs raise the bar when you loosen the wing nuts. When you tighten the wing nuts, the springs collapse into counter-bores on the underside of the bar.

EXPLODED VIEW
EXPANDER

5-6 While most clamps produce compression to hold things together, this *expander* generates tension to force them apart. There is a coupling nut embedded in each handle. As you turn the handles, the coupling nuts move along a threaded rod, pressing out from the ends.

CAMS

Like screws, cams are wound wedges. But instead of winding vertically, a cam wedge winds horizontally around a pivot. (SEE FIGURE 5-7.) As you rotate the cam, its surface bears against any nearby object with increasing pressure, just as if you were driving a wedge between the pivot and that object. You can use this pressure to secure a workpiece or to clamp an assembly together. (SEE FIGURE 5-8.)

5-7 There's a common misconception-tion that a cam is just a disc with an off-center pivot, but it's a little more involved than that. To design a cam, you must first draw a *spiral*, a curve whose radius increases steadily around a central point that will become the pivot. An easy way to do this is to wind a string around a dowel and tie the free end to a pencil. Center the dowel on the pivot mark and swing the pencil around it, unwinding the string. If you want the radius of the spiral to increase slowly, use a small dowel. For one that increases quickly, use a larger dowel. Once you've drawn the spiral, add a *lever* so you can easily rotate the cam. If you want to turn the cam to the same position every time you use it, add a small *flat* at that point in the curve. The flat helps you find the correct position and helps prevent the cam clamp from coming loose.

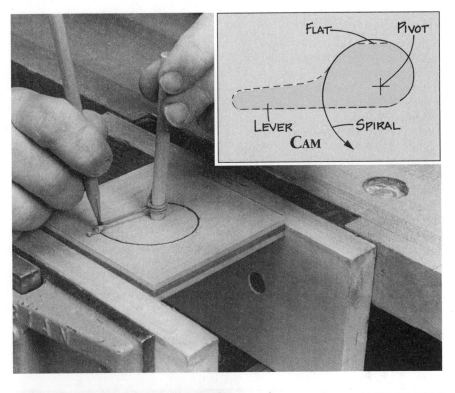

5-8 On this *cam clamp*, a wooden cam moves an adjustable jaw. To tighten the clamp, slide the jaw along the bar until the face contacts the assembly you want to hold together, then throw the cam lever. As the cam rotates, it presses against a thin, flexible finger that has been partially cut from the jaw, forcing the finger to press against the work.

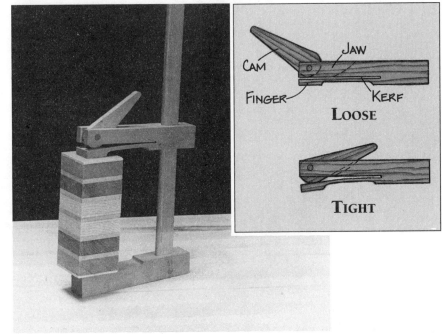

LEVERS

Finally, you can use a lever and a fulcrum to apply clamping pressure. As you press on one end of the lever, it pivots on the fulcrum and the other end presses against an object. The amount of clamping pressure you generate depends on the fulcrum's position and the length of the lever. (*See Figure 5-9.*) The closer the fulcrum is to the working end of the lever and the longer the handle is in proportion to the working end, the greater the *mechanical advantage*. As the mechanical advantage increases, so does the pressure you can apply.

5-9 The amount of clamping pressure you can generate with a lever depends primarily on where you place the fulcrum. (1) If you center the fulcrum between the ends of the lever, the "working end" will press against the wood with the same force you apply to the "handle." Both ends will move the same distance, too. (2) If you move the fulcrum closer to the clamping end, this provides a *mechanical advantage* that magnifies the force you apply. The clamping pressure increases, although the distance the working end travels decreases. (3) If you can't move the fulcrum, you can accomplish the same thing by lengthening the lever. The longer the handle in proportion to the working end, the greater the mechanical advantage.

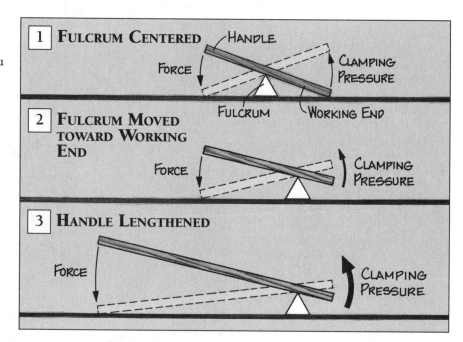

1 FULCRUM CENTERED — HANDLE
FORCE — CLAMPING PRESSURE
FULCRUM — WORKING END

2 FULCRUM MOVED TOWARD WORKING END
FORCE — CLAMPING PRESSURE

3 HANDLE LENGTHENED
FORCE — CLAMPING PRESSURE

A BIT OF ADVICE

Although toggle clamps are convenient, they don't provide a lot of pressure. They are best used in applications where you need a small or medium force to secure the work. When you need more pressure, you can build a much more powerful clamp around a carriage bolt. The shop-made clamp shown does the same job as a toggle clamp but generates more pressure and spreads it over a wider area. It's also less expensive to make than a toggle clamp is to buy.

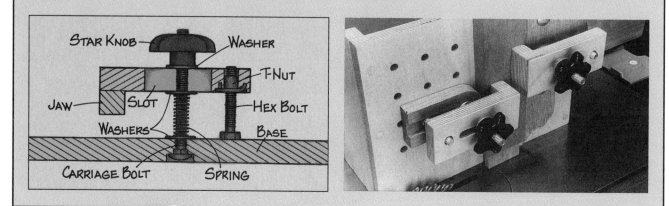

STAR KNOB — WASHER
— T-NUT
JAW — SLOT — HEX BOLT
WASHERS — BASE
CARRIAGE BOLT — SPRING

Levers are most often used in conjunction with other clamping devices. The long-reach C-clamp shown in *Figure 5-4* is a good example — pressure is applied to the screw and transferred to the work through a lever (movable jaw). The protruding handle on a cam and the grip on a ratchet handle are also levers — pressure is applied to a lever and transferred through a cam or screw. The longer these handles are, the greater the mechanical advantage, and the more pressure you can apply.

Except for shave horses and brakes, it's rare to find a shop-made lever clamp used by itself in jig making.

(*See Figure 5-10.*) However, commercially made devices called *toggle clamps* are quite common. (*See Figure 5-11.*) Although the mechanics are slightly more complex, these work on the same principle as a lever and a fulcrum. Several different types of toggle clamps are shown in *Figure 1-11* on page 10.

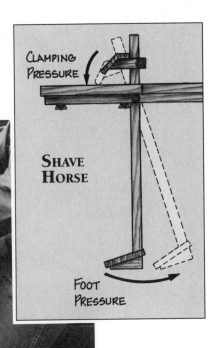

5-10 A *shave horse* is a traditional tool for securing work. This is an updated version — it attaches to your workbench. As you step on the foot pedal, it moves a lever that pivots on a fulcrum. The working end of the lever is attached to a hold-down, which presses down on the work and clamps it to a worktable. To release the hold-down, simply take your foot off the pedal.

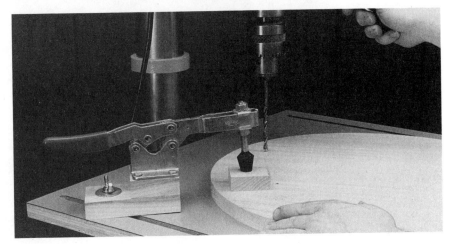

5-11 This *drill press hold-down* incorporates a commercial lever-action toggle clamp. The clamp is mounted on a base which is secured to the drill press table with a carriage bolt. When you throw the lever on the clamp, it holds the work to the table. **Note:** You can easily modify this design to make a hold-down for another power tool or your workbench.

VACUUM CLAMPS

Once used exclusively in industrial applications, vacuum-operated clamps became more common in small woodworking shops as new technologies made them less expensive. They offer significant advantages over traditional mechanical clamps for many woodworking operations, particularly those that require hold-downs. Compared to their mechanical counterparts, vacuum clamps are often easier to build and set up, quicker to operate, smaller and lighter, and less likely to get in your way.

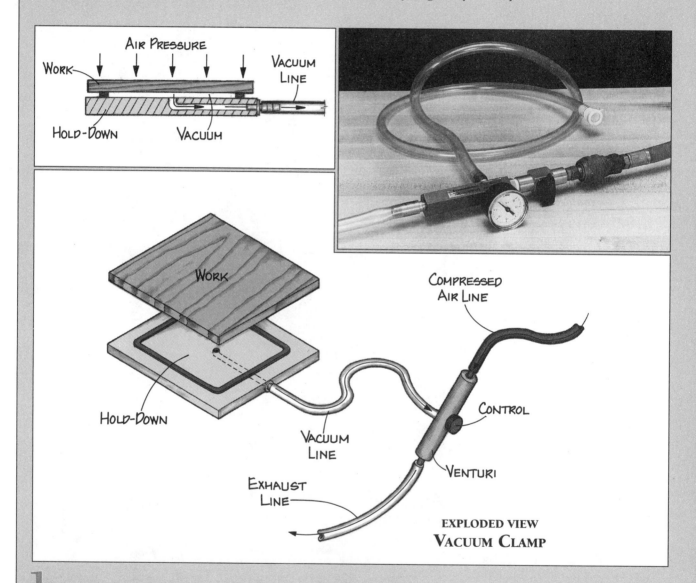

EXPLODED VIEW
VACUUM CLAMP

1 **Vacuum clamps use the** weight of the atmosphere to generate clamping pressure. The air around us presses in from all sides. When you create a vacuum on one side of a board, you remove the air pressure from that side only. The pressure that remains on the other side presses the board toward the vacuum with a force of up to 1,800 pounds per square foot. To create the necessary vacuum, hook an air compressor to a special valve called a *venturi*. The venturi forces the air to move very quickly. The pressure plummets inside the fast-moving air stream and a partial vacuum forms. The venturi shown is hand activated, but there are also foot-activated models available.

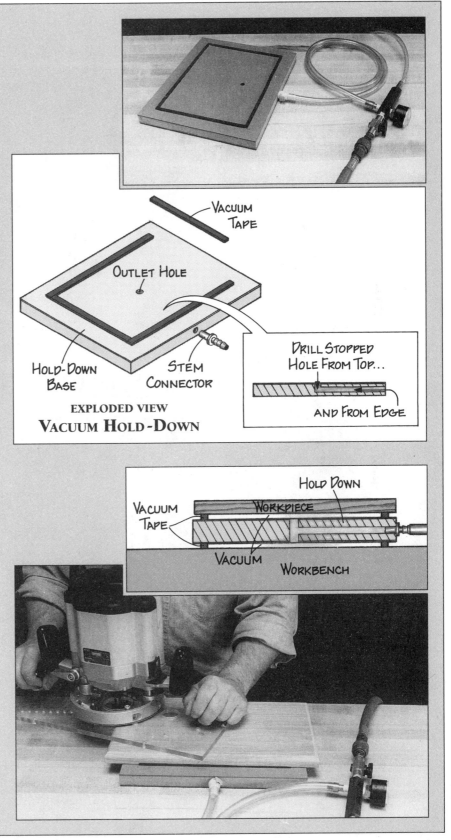

VACUUM TAPE

OUTLET HOLE

HOLD-DOWN BASE

STEM CONNECTOR

EXPLODED VIEW
VACUUM HOLD-DOWN

DRILL STOPPED HOLE FROM TOP...

AND FROM EDGE

HOLD DOWN

VACUUM TAPE

WORKPIECE

VACUUM

WORKBENCH

2 **To build a *vacuum hold-down*,** cut a flat sheet of a nonporous material large enough to support the work. Plastics, laminate-covered MDF, and dense, closed-grain hardwoods work best. Drill a hole in the board for an air outlet and install a stem connector in the hole. Finally, attach dense sponge rubber *vacuum tape* around the perimeter of the board to create an air seal. Hook the vacuum line to the connector, place a board on top of the hold-down, and activate the venturi. A vacuum forms between the board and the hold-down inside the area outlined by the vacuum tape. In a few seconds, the board is secure.

3 **There are many variations on** this basic vacuum clamp design. You can cut the hold-down board to any shape you want, simple or complex. You can also drill the edge of the hold-down material to create an air outlet that opens to both the top and the bottom faces. Put vacuum tape around both surfaces, and the vacuum will secure the hold-down to your workbench as well as hold the work.

(continued) ▷

VACUUM CLAMPS — CONTINUED

4 **Make a multipurpose hold-**down by applying several concentric rings of vacuum tape to a large, flat surface, sizing the rings to accommodate different workpieces. Cut ½-inch-wide openings between the rings to provide a path for the air to be evacuated. Use a 1-inch-long piece of tape as a "gate" to close the opening on the largest ring you want to use.

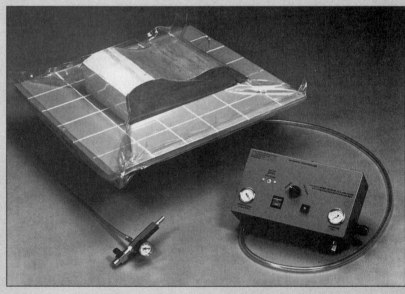

5 **By using a *vacuum bag,* you** can create a veneer press that will clamp veneer to both flat and curved surfaces. Apply glue to the core material and position the veneer on the core. Slip the assembly into the bag, seal it, and hook up the vacuum hose. When you activate the venturi, a vacuum forms inside the bag. The air on the outside presses against the bag and the assembly, evenly distributing the pressure across the entire surface. **Note:** Do not apply water-based glues directly to the veneer; they may curl or wrinkle before you can clamp them in place.

WHERE TO FIND IT

You can purchase vacuum clamping materials from either of these sources:

CMT Tools
310 Mears Boulevard
Oldsmar, FL 34677

Quality VAKuum Products
43 Bradford Street
Concord, MA 01742

SPECIAL HOLDING JIGS

Most of the clamping devices shown so far were designed to hold simple boards with flat surfaces and straight edges. How do you hold unusually shaped workpieces such as lathe turnings or scroll-sawed figures? To fit them, you may have to build a special cradle or form.

HOLDING TURNINGS AND DOWELS

There are two ways to hold cylindrical shapes such as lathe turnings and dowels. The simplest and most common is a *V-jig* — a flat, straight board with a V-shaped groove in one face. The cylinder rests in the groove. (SEE FIGURE 5-12.) To secure the cylinder in a V-jig, use straps. (SEE FIGURE 5-13.)

You can also hold these workpieces between two pointed *centers*, much like those used on a lathe. This arrangement is especially useful for holding turnings with coves and beads of various diameters. These turnings may not rest horizontally in a V-shaped groove — instead, they will sit at an angle. Suspending the turnings between centers prevents this problem.

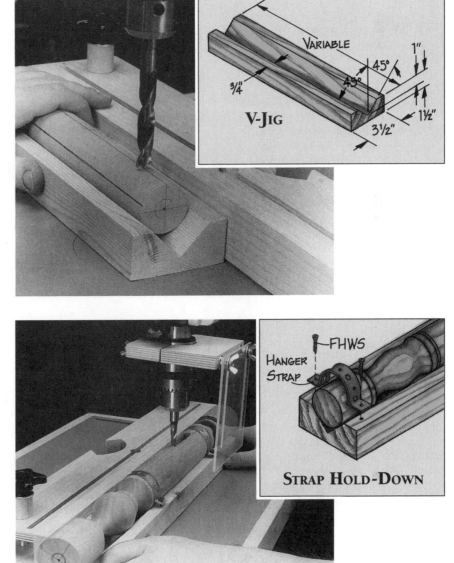

5-12 A V-jig cradles a cylindrical workpiece, such as a lathe turning or a dowel, holding it horizontally. To make the jig shown, cut a V-shaped groove down the length of a two-by-four scrap.

5-13 To secure a turning or a dowel in a V-jig, use a pair of *strap hold-downs*, one near each end. Make the straps from short lengths of hanger strap, a metal banding sold in the plumbing section of most hardware stores to support pipes. Bend the straps to fit the workpiece and fasten them to the V-jig with flat-head wood screws. Bend each strap so the ends don't quite touch the jig. As you tighten the screws that fasten them, the straps will press down on the work, clamping it in place.

Make the centers from nails or screws. Or, grind points on the ends of bolts or threaded rods. Mount the centers in wooden supports and attach the supports to a rigid base. To secure a turning in this fixture, drive the pointed centers toward one another, squeezing the wood between them. (SEE FIGURE 5-14.)

HOLDING INTRICATE SHAPES

To hold an irregularly shaped workpiece, a *notch jig* often works best. You can make this jig by sawing a cutout in a scrap of wood to fit the shape you wish to hold. Then place the workpiece inside the cutout. (SEE FIGURE 5-15.)

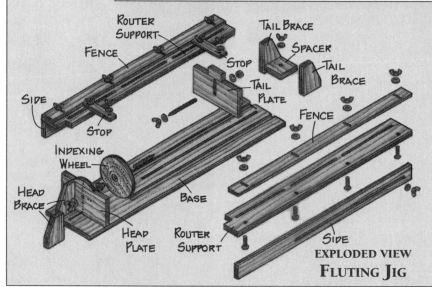

5-14 This *fluting jig* lets you rout flutes, reeds, and similar shapes in a spindle turning. The turning mounts between two adjustable centers made from threaded rod. An indexing wheel fits over one center and screws to the end of the turning. This wheel has holes around its circumference, evenly spaced a precise number of degrees apart. By inserting a pin through one of these holes and into the support, you prevent the turning from rotating. To "index" the turning — rotate it a precise number of degrees — remove the pin, rotate the work until the next hole in the indexing wheel lines up with the hole in the support, and replace the pin.

ROUTER SUPPORT

FENCE

TAIL BRACE

SPACER

STOP

TAIL BRACE

SIDE

TAIL PLATE

STOP

FENCE

INDEXING WHEEL

HEAD BRACE

BASE

HEAD PLATE

ROUTER SUPPORT

SIDE

EXPLODED VIEW
FLUTING JIG

5-15 Use a *notch jig* to hold odd-shaped workpieces and assemblies. Cut a notch in a scrap the same size and shape as the work, and place the work inside the notch. The notch jig can be fixed or moving, depending on the application. Both the jigs shown hold mitered boards. The *sliding notch jig* (left) feeds the boards into a disc sander, while the *stationary notch jig* (right) is clamped to a drill press table to position the boards under the bit. **Note:** If the work must be secured in the notch, use a simple clamping device such as a wedge or a toggle clamp.

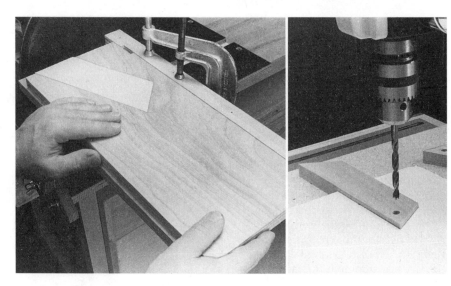

ASSEMBLY JIGS

An assembly jig is a frame or a form that holds the parts of a project in the proper relationship to each other. These fixtures come in handy when:

■ The parts of a project must be positioned accurately

■ You need to maintain square corners or precise angles

■ The parts are difficult to hold and clamp otherwise

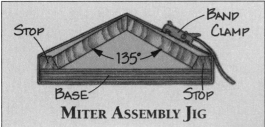

MITER ASSEMBLY JIG

5-16 This specialized assembly jig holds two boards with beveled edges at a 135-degree angle to one another. The outside edges of the boards butt against long stops. The stops are fastened to a base to keep them a specific distance apart. Band clamps hold the boards in the jig and squeeze the beveled edges together at the same time.

CORNER JIGS AND CLAMPS

One of the most useful assembly fixtures is a *corner jig*. This workshop aid holds two parts at the proper angle to one another for both temporary and permanent assembly. Use it to hold the parts in position while fitting them together, while driving screws or nails, or while glue is drying.

Most corner jigs are simple brackets that fasten the parts of the assembly, as shown in *FIGURE 1-17* on page 14. You can also make a frame or a cradle to hold the parts at the proper angle. *(SEE FIGURE 5-16.)* If you wish, add built-in clamps to a bracket or a frame to make a *corner clamp*. *(SEE FIGURE 5-17.)*

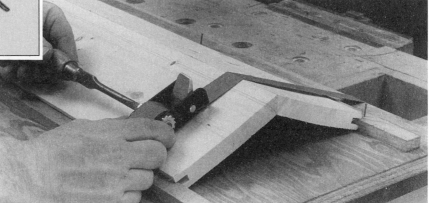

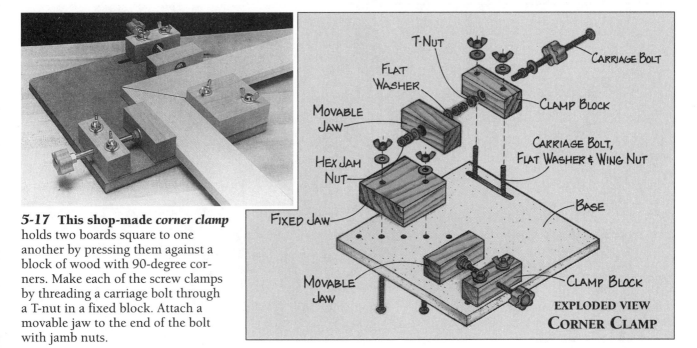

5-17 This shop-made *corner clamp* holds two boards square to one another by pressing them against a block of wood with 90-degree corners. Make each of the screw clamps by threading a carriage bolt through a T-nut in a fixed block. Attach a movable jaw to the end of the bolt with jamb nuts.

EXPLODED VIEW
CORNER CLAMP

CLAMPING GRIDS

When putting together odd-shaped frames, panels, and other flat assemblies, a *clamping grid* comes in handy. Make the grid from strips of hardwood. Lap the strips so the spaces between them are 2 to 3 inches square — large enough to insert a small clamp. Then, instead of clamping the parts to one another, clamp them to the grid to hold them in position. (*See Figure 5-18.*)

You can also make a corner assembly jig to hold three-dimensional assemblies. Two clamping grids, joined at right angles with corner clamps, provide a framework on which you can assemble the corner of a project that might otherwise be impossible to clamp together. (*See Figure 5-19.*) Join four clamping grids to make a gridwork box, and you can assemble the entire structure inside the box. Or make a specially shaped frame to support the parts. Just remember to plan for release — you must be able to get the project out of the grid or the frame once it's assembled.

5-18 Use a *clamping grid* to help assemble odd-shaped frames and other unusual assemblies that are difficult to clamp. Instead of trying to clamp the parts together, fasten them to the grid and let the grid hold them together.

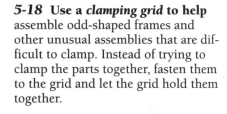

5-19 This *corner assembly jig* holds the scroll-sawed sides of a delicate corner shelf to help fit the parts and glue them together. It's made from two scraps of plywood joined at right angles. Each piece of plywood has been drilled with rows of large holes to create a grid. The holes are large enough to insert small clamps through the grid.

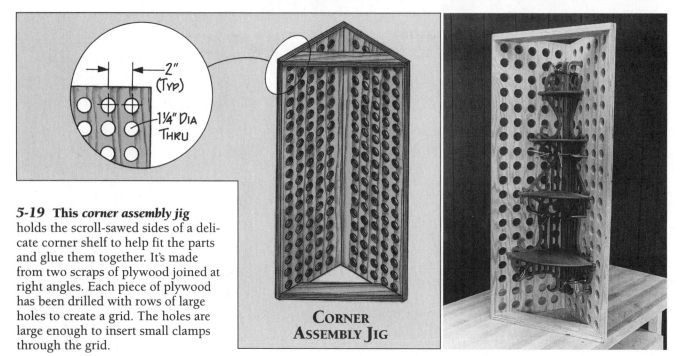

PROJECTS

6

A Craftsman's Dozen: 12 Jigs and Fixtures You Cannot Work Without

Many jigs and fixtures are designed for a single woodworking operation or built for a specific woodworking project. I have found some, however, that can be used over and over again for a variety of tasks and projects. Within this group, an even dozen have proved so useful that I find them indispensable to the woodworking I like to do. Once I built them, I wondered how I ever got along without them.

Auxiliary Fence

Universal Featherboard

Adjustable-Height Fence

Tilting Drill Press Table

Support Stand

Lift-Top Router Table

Router Height Adjustor

Sliding Cutoff Table

Pusher

Knock-Down Cutting Grid

Circular Saw Guide

Tenoning Jig

1. PUSHER

You absolutely, positively cannot do without push sticks and push shoes. And you need both — a push stick lets you manipulate the work close to a cutter, while a push shoe holds it flat against a table or a fence. Many experienced woodworkers keep a pair of these safety devices at every work station so they can choose the proper tool for each operation. Sometimes they find it necessary to switch during a task.

This simple *pusher* serves as both a push stick *and* a push shoe so you always have the right tool on hand. Use the notch on the nose when you need to reach in close to a cutter (A). Or, use the heel to feed the work and hold it down (B). Additionally, this tool has a unique V-groove running the length of the sole. Place the groove over a corner of a board to hold it against both the table and the fence as you feed it (C).

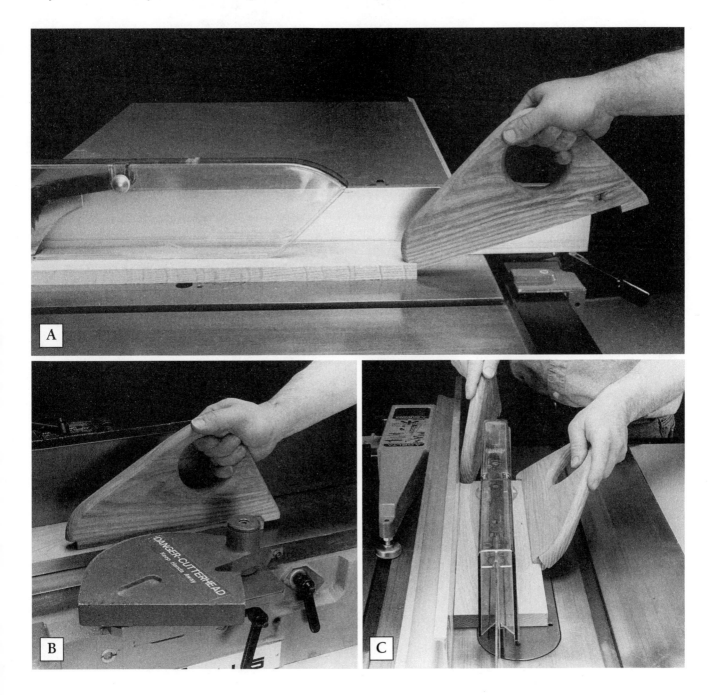

MATERIALS LIST
(FINISHED DIMENSIONS)

Parts

A. Body $\frac{3}{4}''$ x 5 $\frac{3}{4}''$ x 12″
B. Heel $\frac{1}{2}''$ x $\frac{3}{4}''$ x 1″

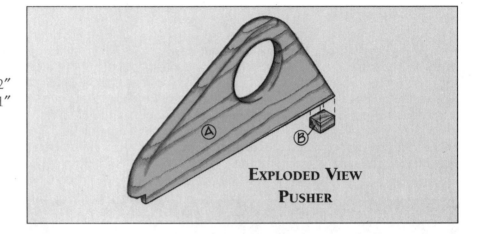

EXPLODED VIEW
PUSHER

PLAN OF PROCEDURE

1 Select the stock and cut the parts. Select a scrap of hardwood or plywood to make the body and the heel, then cut them to size.

2 Cut the body profile. Lay out the body profile, as shown in the *Side View*. Create the handle hole with a 3-inch-diameter hole saw, and cut the outside profile with a band saw, scroll saw, or saber saw. Sand the sawed edges smooth.

3 Cut the groove and round the edges. Using a table-mounted router and a V-groove bit, cut the stopped V-groove in the sole, as shown in the *End View*. Then round the top edges of the body and the inside edges of the handle with a $\frac{3}{8}$-inch roundover bit. Sand the rounded edges smooth.

4 Assemble and finish the pusher. Glue the heel to the sole so the back ends are flush. When the glue is dry, finish sand the pusher and apply a finish.

A BIT OF ADVICE

Don't make just one pusher. While you're set up, make several — two for the table saw, two for the jointer, and one each for the remaining stationary power tools in your shop. That way, there will always be a pusher at hand when you need one.

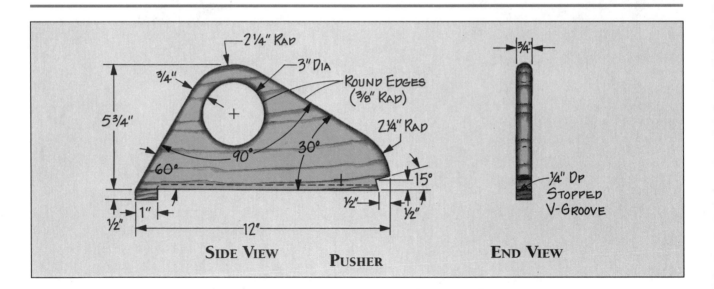

SIDE VIEW   **PUSHER**   **END VIEW**

2. AUXILIARY FENCE

One of the most versatile jigs I've ever run across is a simple wooden T-square. It can be used as a guide or backstop for dozens of operations, with the crossbar automatically squaring the straightedge to the edge of the work. The trouble is, you have to fuss with clamps to fasten it down. So I added a built-in clamp to make it more convenient to use.

My improved T-square, more properly called an *auxiliary fence,* fastens to any flat surface up to 30 inches wide. Just turn the crank behind the crossbar — this drives a movable jaw, gripping the work between the jaw and the crossbar. Use it as a guide for portable power tool operations (*A*), or as an extra fence on stationary power tools (*B*).

A long T-slot in the top lets you mount stops and other accessories to the fence (*C*). It also allows you to use the fence as a mounting bar for jigs such as the "Universal Featherboard" on page 69.

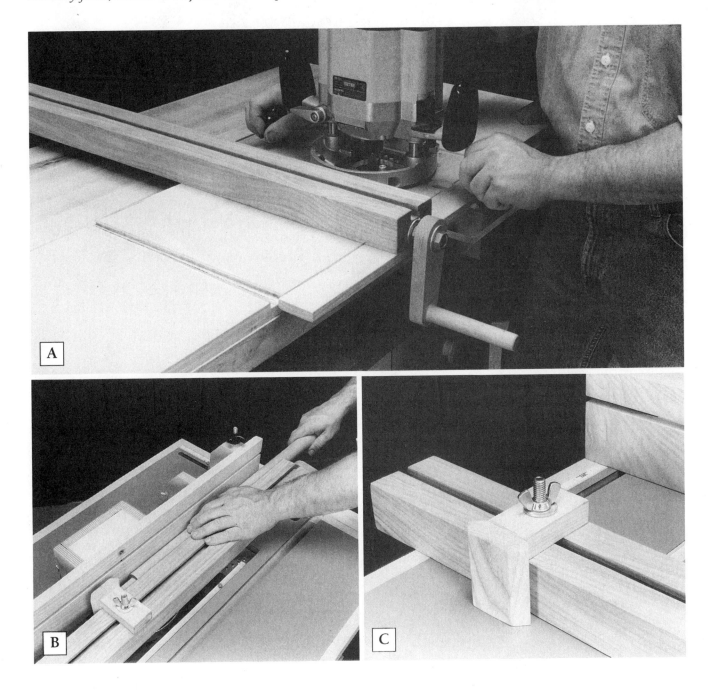

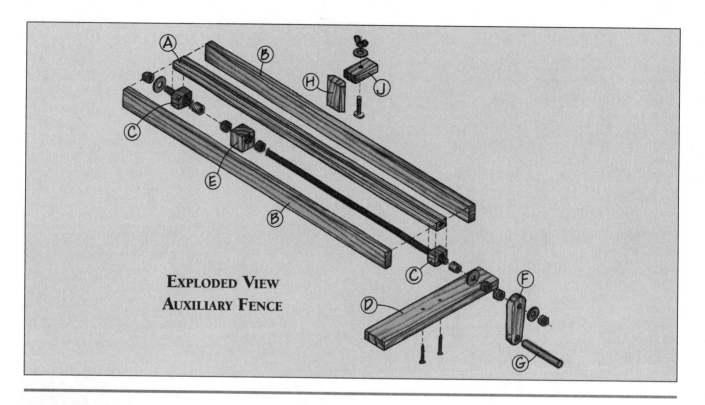

**EXPLODED VIEW
AUXILIARY FENCE**

MATERIALS LIST (FINISHED DIMENSIONS)

Parts

A.	Top	¾" x 1¼" x 33¾"
B.	Sides (2)	¾" x 1¾" x 33¾"
C.	Ends (2)	1" x 1¼" x ¾"
D.	Crossbar	½" x 1¾" x 14"
E.	Movable jaw	1" x 1¼" x 1½"
F.	Crank arm	¾" x 1¾" x 5"
G.	Crank handle	¾" dia. x 5"
H.	Stop (optional)	¾" x 2¼" x 2½"
J.	Stop mount (optional)	¾" x 1½" x 2¾"

Hardware

#8 x 1½" Flathead wood
   screws (4, plus 2 optional)
½"-13 x 36" Threaded rod
⁵⁄₁₆" x 2" Flange bolt (optional)
⁷⁄₁₆" Flat washers (3)*
⁵⁄₁₆" Flat washer (optional)
½" Jamb nuts (5)
½" Stop nut
⁵⁄₁₆" Wing nut (optional)
½" I.D. x ¹¹⁄₁₆" O.D. x ¾"
   Bushings (2)†

*One-size-smaller washers often fit a rod
or a bolt with less play than same-size
washers.
†You can also use short sections of
½" I.D. iron plumbing pipe instead of
bushings.

PLAN OF PROCEDURE

1 **Select the stock and cut the parts to size.** To make the auxiliary fence, you'll need approximately 2 board feet of clear, straight-grained 4/4 (four-quarters) hardwood and a 5-inch-long scrap of ¾-inch-diameter dowel. Plane the stock to ¾ inch thick and cut all the parts except the crossbar, movable jaw, and ends. If you elect to make the stop, double-miter its edges, as shown in the *Stop/Top View*. (The miters keep sawdust from interfering with the work.)

Plane the remaining stock to ½ inch thick and cut the crossbar. Glue two ½-inch-thick scraps face to face to make 1-inch-thick stock for the movable jaw and ends. Let the glue dry, then cut these parts.

Note: The grain direction in the top, sides, and ends must all run in the same direction (horizontal) so they expand and contract together. The grain in the movable jaw must be perpendicular (vertical) to them for strength.

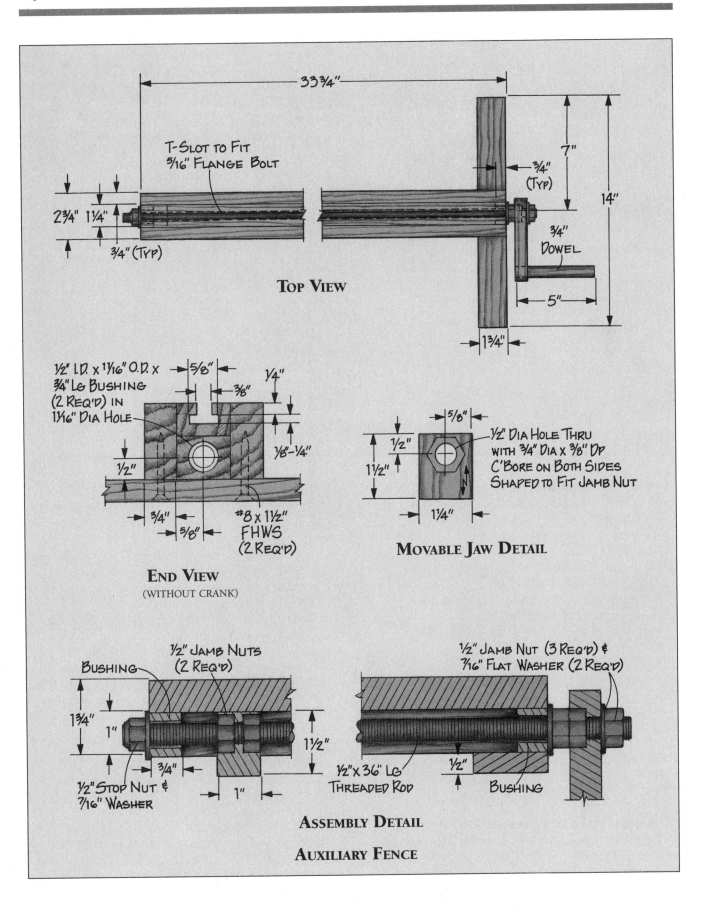

TOP VIEW

END VIEW

(WITHOUT CRANK)

MOVABLE JAW DETAIL

ASSEMBLY DETAIL

AUXILIARY FENCE

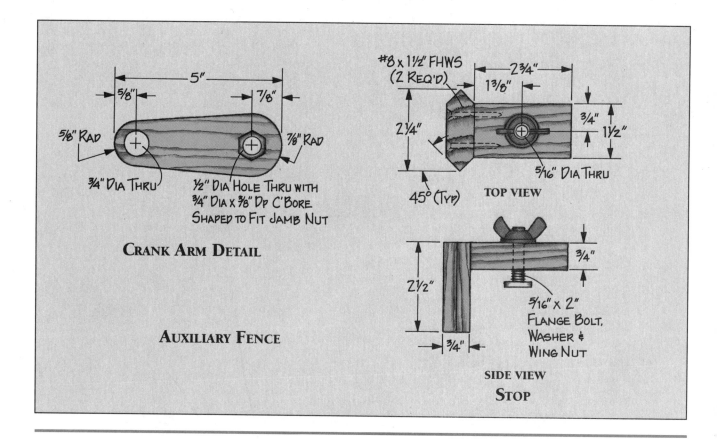

CRANK ARM DETAIL

AUXILIARY FENCE

TOP VIEW

SIDE VIEW
STOP

2 Cut the slot in the top. Using a T-slot cutter, rout a mounting slot for a ⁵⁄₁₆-inch flange bolt in the top, as shown in the *Top View* and the *End View.*

3 Drill the holes. Lay out and drill these holes:
■ ¾-inch-diameter hole in the crank arm, as shown in the *Crank Arm Detail*
■ ¹¹⁄₁₆-inch-diameter holes in the ends for the bushings, as shown in the *End View*
■ ½-inch-diameter counterbored hole in crank arm
■ ½-inch-diameter hole counterbored on *both sides* in the movable jaw, as shown in the *Movable Jaw Detail*
■ ⁵⁄₁₆-inch-diameter hole in the stop mount, as shown in the *Stop/Top View*
Using a chisel, enlarge the counterbores in the crank arm and the movable jaw to fit hexagonal jamb nuts. Don't press the nuts into the counterbores — you want a fairly loose fit.

4 Assemble the fence and the stop. Glue the bushings in the ends with a cyanoacrylate adhesive such as Super Glue. Assemble the top, sides, and ends with wood glue. Also glue the crank handle in the crank arm and the stop to the stop mount. Let the glue dry, then joint the sides straight and finish sand the assembly. Attach the crossbar with flathead wood screws, making sure it's square to the sides. (Do *not* glue the crossbar in place. It will get chewed up, especially if you use the jig as a routing guide, and you will want to replace it.)

Attach the crank assembly to one end of the threaded rod with washers and jamb nuts, as shown in the *Assembly Detail.* Insert jamb nuts in the movable stop and try threading the ½-inch-diameter rod through them. If the rod binds, rotate one of the nuts ⅙ turn and try again. When you find a position that allows the rod to turn easily, install the rod and the jaw in the fence assembly. Do *not* glue the nuts in the jaw. Secure the rod in the fence with a stop nut and a washer.

Install a flange bolt, washer, and wing nut in the stop and, if applicable, check that the stop mounts easily in the fence's T-slot.

5 Finish the fence and the stop. When you're satisfied that the fence and stop work properly, remove all the hardware and do any necessary sanding. Apply a finish to all wood surfaces and reassemble.

3. Universal Featherboard

Featherboards hold the work against a fence or down on a table as you feed it past a blade or cutter, making the operation safer and more accurate. They are essential shop aids, but they're a pain in the neck to mount and adjust — once again, you have to fuss with clamps. When I found the Auxiliary Fence (see page 65) could be easily fastened to most stationary power tools, I built a featherboard system that would mount on the fence.

This *universal featherboard* system includes two featherboards that can be arranged at different angles and in different configurations to fit the operation. A brace holds the featherboards at the proper angle and brackets mount the system to the fence. You can use both featherboards horizontally, positioning them to press against the work before and after the cutter (A). Or, mount one horizontally and clamp the other vertically to hold the work against the fence and the table at the same time (B). You can even set up the featherboards to press against the work several inches above the table (C). This helps hold wide panels against a tall fence.

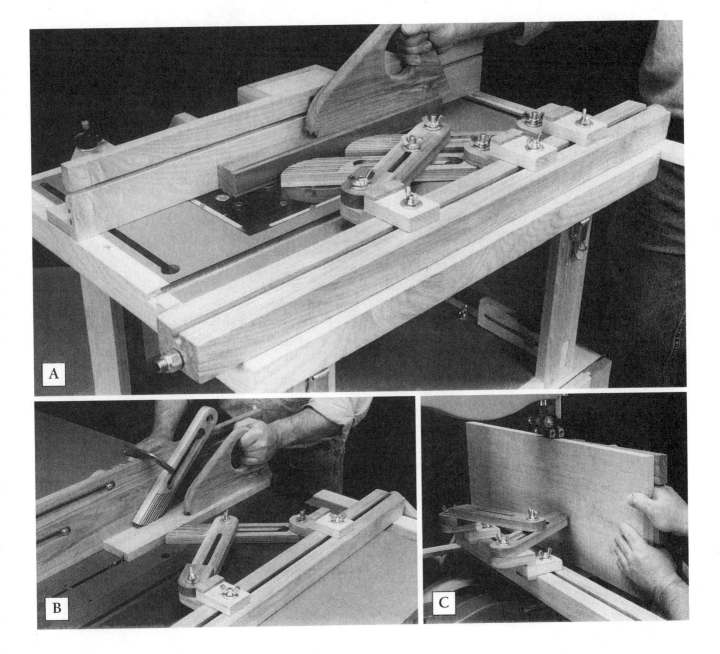

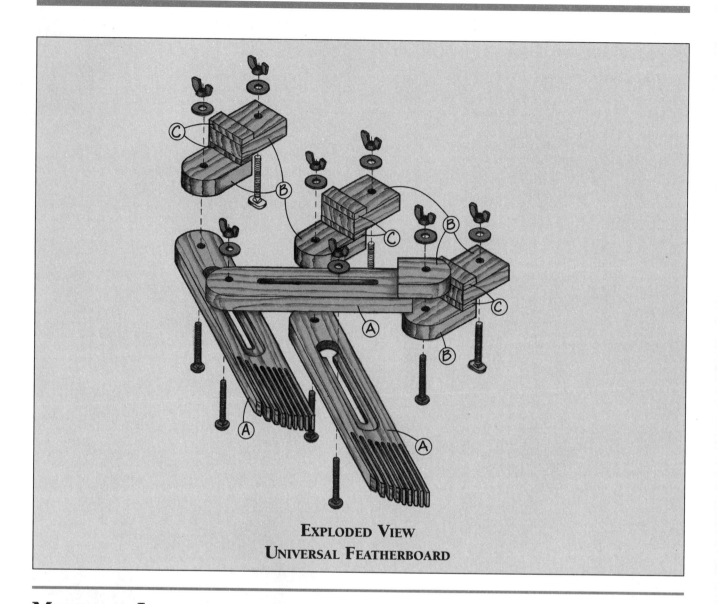

EXPLODED VIEW
UNIVERSAL FEATHERBOARD

MATERIALS LIST (FINISHED DIMENSIONS)

Parts

A. Featherboards/
   Brace (3)   ¾" x 2⅛" x 12"
B. Mounts (7)   ¾" x 2⅛" x 3"
C. Spacers (6)   ¼" x ¾" x 2⅛"

Hardware

⁵⁄₁₆" x 2" Carriage bolts (5)
⁵⁄₁₆" x 2" Flange bolts (3)
⁵⁄₁₆" Flat washers (8)
⁵⁄₁₆" Wing nuts (8)

PLAN OF PROCEDURE

1 Select the stock and cut the parts. You can make this featherboard system from scraps of ¾-inch-thick hardwood, as long as the grain is straight and clear. Cut the parts to the sizes specified in the Materials List.

2 Cut the feathers. Create the "feathers" in the featherboards on a band saw by cutting ⅛-inch-wide kerfs evenly spaced ⅛ inch apart. You can also use a scroll saw or a saber saw.

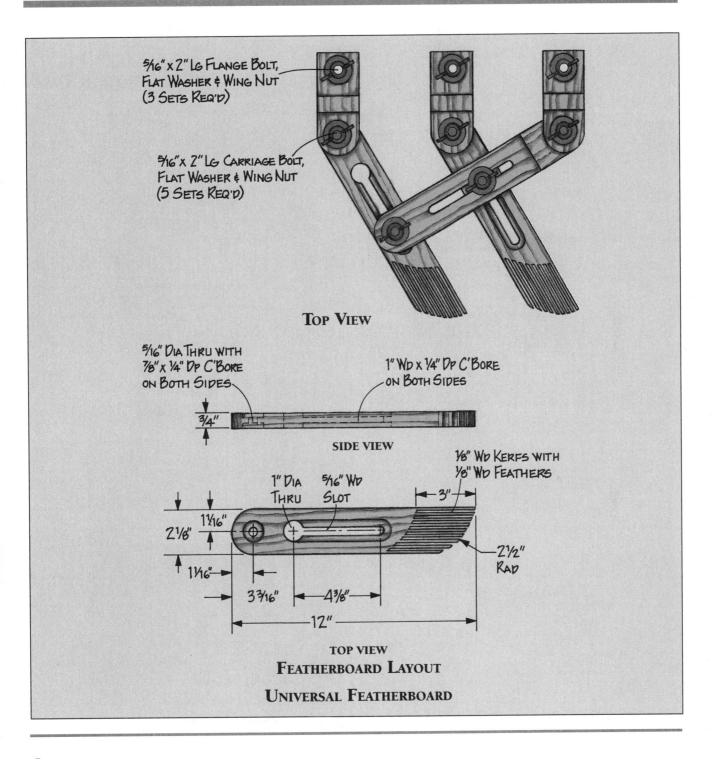

5/16" x 2" Lg Flange Bolt, Flat Washer & Wing Nut (3 Sets Req'd)

5/16" x 2" Lg Carriage Bolt, Flat Washer & Wing Nut (5 Sets Req'd)

Top View

5/16" Dia Thru with 7/8" x 1/4" Dp C'Bore on Both Sides

1" Wd x 1/4" Dp C'Bore on Both Sides

3/4"

SIDE VIEW

1/8" Wd Kerfs with 1/8" Wd Feathers

1" Dia Thru

5/16" Wd Slot

3"

1 11/16"

2 1/8"

1 1/16"

2 1/2" Rad

3 3/16"

4 3/8"

12"

TOP VIEW
FEATHERBOARD LAYOUT

UNIVERSAL FEATHERBOARD

3 Drill the holes. Lay out the featherboards, brace, and mounts. Then drill these holes:
■ 1-inch-diameter access holes through the featherboards, as shown in the *Featherboard Layout/Top View*
■ 5/16-inch-diameter holes, counterbored on both sides, in the ends of the featherboards
■ 5/16-inch-diameter holes in the ends of the brace

and the mounts, as shown in the *Brace Layout/Top View* and *Mounting Bracket Layout/Top View*

4 Rout the slots. Rout 5/16-inch-wide slots with 1-inch-wide counterbores in the featherboards. (Note that these slots are counterbored on *both* sides.) Also rout a 5/16-inch-wide slot in the brace.

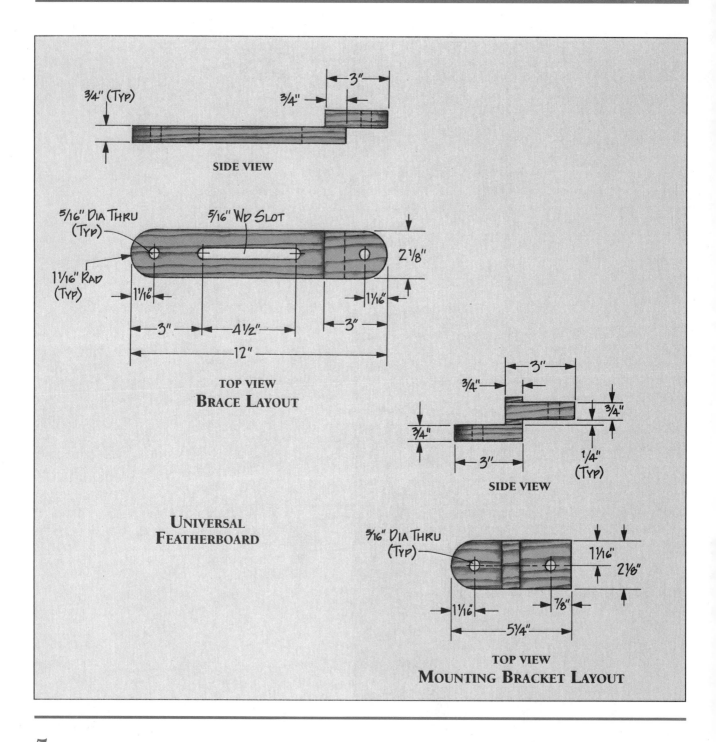

3"

3/4" (TYP)

3/4"

SIDE VIEW

5/16" DIA THRU
(TYP)

5/16" WD SLOT

1 1/16" RAD
(TYP)

2 1/8"

1 1/16"

1 1/16"

3"   4 1/2"   3"

12"

TOP VIEW
BRACE LAYOUT

**UNIVERSAL
FEATHERBOARD**

3"

3/4"

3/4"

3/4"

1/4"
(TYP)

3"

SIDE VIEW

5/16" DIA THRU
(TYP)

1 1/16"

2 1/8"

1 1/16"

7/8"

5 1/4"

TOP VIEW
MOUNTING BRACKET LAYOUT

5 Cut the profiles. Cut the profiles of the feather-boards, brace, and mounts with a band saw, scroll saw, or saber saw. Sand the sawed edges smooth. **Note:** Only four of the seven mounts have round profiles on one end; the other three remain square.

6 Assemble and finish the featherboard system. Finish sand all the parts. Glue a mount to the brace.

Also glue the remaining mounts and spacers together to make three mounting brackets. Let the glue dry, then assemble the universal featherboard system and install it on the auxiliary fence. When you're satisfied the parts work together properly, take it apart and remove the hardware. Do any necessary touch-up sanding, then apply a finish to all wooden surfaces. Reassemble the featherboard system.

4. SUPPORT STAND

An adjustable support stand is an essential safety tool in a one-man shop. It becomes that extra pair of hands you need to safely handle large or long work-pieces.

This particular stand is "omnidirectional" — the roller bearings rotate in any direction, allowing you to use the stand for ripping, crosscutting, and even circle-cutting (A). The three-legged support ensures that it will always sit solidly on the floor. And it adjusts from 30 to 46½ inches high — just a little bit lower and a little bit higher than the work surfaces in my shop. (You can customize the height range for your own shop simply by changing the length of the support, support sides, post, and slot in the post.)

I've also added two unique features. First, the stand is *microadjustable*. A small screw jack rests in the dadoes in the support sides (B). The top of this jack turns on a ⅜-16 carriage bolt. Every turn raises or lowers the roller bearings exactly ⅟16 inch. A half-turn changes the height ⅟32 inch; a quarter-turn, ⅟64 inch. This makes it a simple matter to dial in the height you need. You can also change the height in precise incre-ments when using the stand with a planer or jointer.

Second, the stand has a built-in worktable exten-sion (C). This extension swings up and hooks into a ledger on the power tool (D). When the extension is horizontal, the surface is just a fraction of an inch below the tops of the bearings. I've made several ledgers and attached them to most of my power tools — this lets me add a table extension wherever I need it.

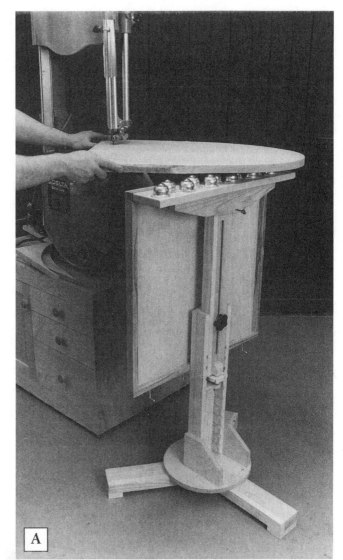

A

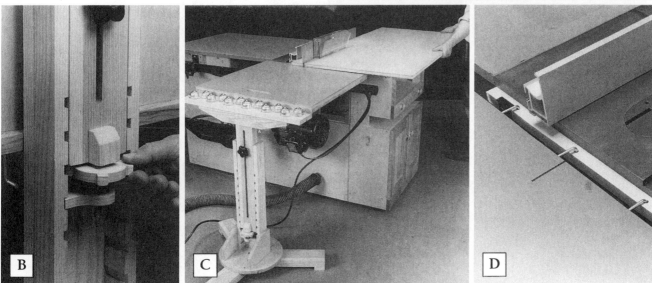

B

C

D

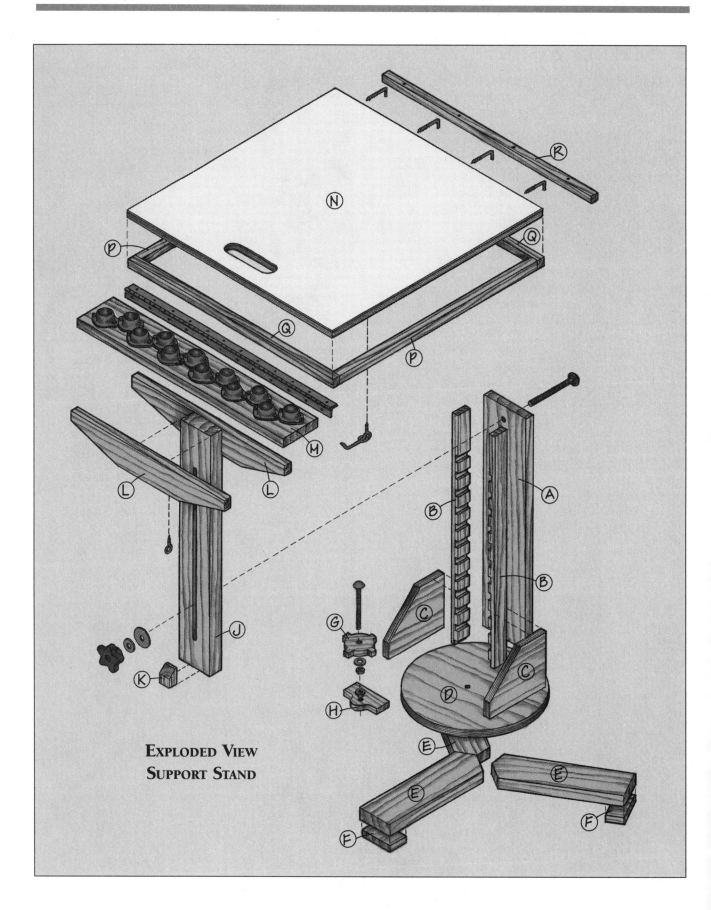

**EXPLODED VIEW
SUPPORT STAND**

MATERIALS LIST (FINISHED DIMENSIONS)

Parts

Base

A.	Support	¾" x 5" x 22½"
B.	Support sides (2)	¾" x 1½" x 22½"
C.	Support braces* (2)	¾" x 5" x 7¼"
D.	Base*	¾" x 12" dia.
E.	Legs (3)	1½" x 3½" x 14"
F.	Feet (3)	¾" x 2" x 3½"
G.	Jack top	½" x 2⅞" x 2⅞"
H.	Jack base	½" x 2¼" x 3¹⁵⁄₁₆"

Stand/Table

J.	Post	1½" x 3½" x 23½"
K.	Adjustment ledge	¾" x 1¼" x 1½"
L.	Platform braces (2)	¾" x 2½" x 18"
M.	Platform	¾" x 4" x 24"
N.	Table extension*	½" x 24" x 24"

P.	Stiles (2)	(variable)† x ¾" x 22½"
Q.	Rails (2)	(variable)† x ¾" x 24"
R.	Ledgers (variable)	¾" x ¾" x 24"

Hardware

Base

#10 x 2½" Flathead wood screws (6)

#10 x 1½" Flathead wood screws (6)

⅜" x 3" Carriage bolt

⅜" x 2½" Carriage bolt

⅜" Flat washers (2)

⅜" Fender washer

⅜" Hex nut

⅜" T-nut

⅜" Star knob

Stand/Table

#10 x 1½" Flathead wood screws (6)

1" Roller bearings and mounting screws (12)

1" x 24" Piano hinge and mounting screws

3" Hook and eye

2½" L-hooks (4)

25" x 25" Plastic laminate sheet (optional)

*Make these parts from plywood.
†Adjust these dimensions so the combined thickness of the table extension assembly is approximately ¹⁄₁₆ inch less than the height of the roller bearings.

PLAN OF PROCEDURE

1 Select the stock and cut the parts. To make this support stand, you need approximately 4 board feet of 8/4 (eight-quarters) hardwood, 5 board feet of 4/4 (four-quarters) hardwood, a 12-inch by 24-inch piece of ¾-inch plywood, and a 24-inch by 24-inch piece of ½-inch plywood.

Plane the 8/4 stock to 1½ inches thick and the 4/4 stock to ¾ inch thick. Cut a small piece from the ¾-inch-thick stock, large enough to make the jack top and jack base, and plane it to ½ inch thick. (Make sure the piece is long enough to plane safely.) Then cut all the parts to size, except for the support sides. For these, cut a board ¾ inch thick, 3½ inches wide, and 22½ inches long and set it aside.

If you wish, cover the top face of the table extension with plastic laminate and chamfer the edges. This will make the surface more durable and reduce friction. (Remember to cover the underside with polyurethane or enamel paint *immediately* to keep the surface from warping.) Lay out the shapes of the base, jack top, and jack base, along with the locations of all holes, slots, and dadoes.

2 Drill the holes. Use your drill press to create these holes:

■ 1¼-inch-diameter holes to mark the ends of the handhold slot in the table extension, as shown in the *Table Extension and Ledger Layout*

■ ⁷⁄₁₆-inch-diameter counterbored hole through the jack base, as shown in the *Jack Base Layout*

■ ⅜-inch-diameter hole through the support near the top end, as shown in the *Base/Back View*

■ ⅜-inch-diameter hole through the jack top, as shown in the *Jack Top Layout*

■ ¼-inch-diameter holes through the ledgers, as shown in the *Table Extension and Ledger Layout*

3 Cut the slots, rabbets, and dadoes. Using a saber saw or a coping saw, remove the waste between the holes in the table extension to create the handhold slot. Rout the ⅜-inch-wide slot in the post, as shown in the *Stand/Table/Back View*. Rout or cut the ½-inch-wide rabbet and dadoes for the jack in the support side stock, then rip the stock into two 1½-inch-wide pieces.

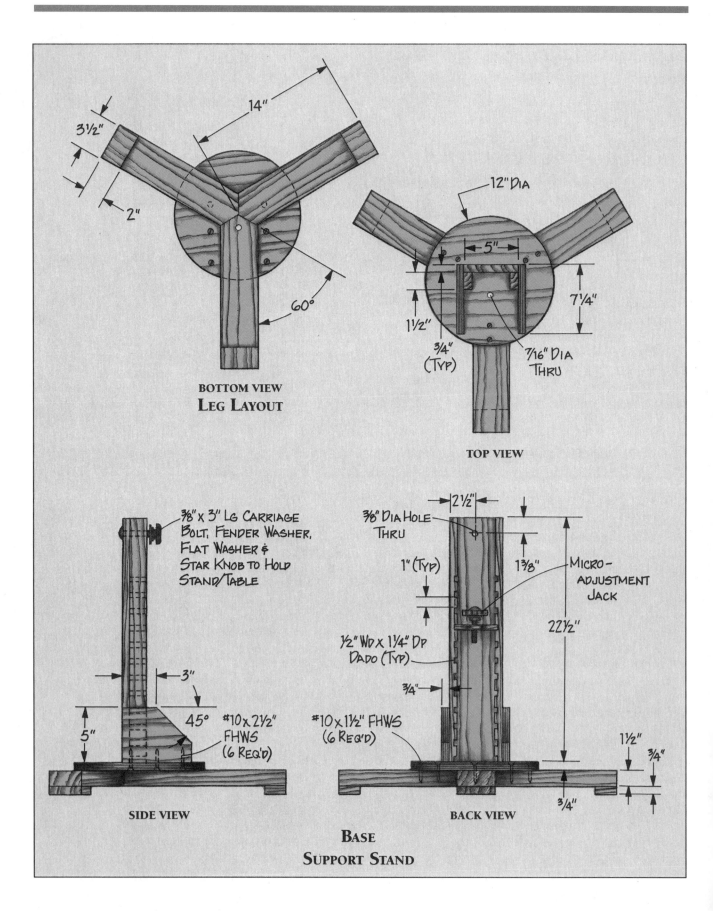

14"

3½"

2"

60°

BOTTOM VIEW
LEG LAYOUT

12" DIA

5"

7¼"

1½"

¾" (TYP)

7/16" DIA THRU

TOP VIEW

⅜" x 3" LG CARRIAGE BOLT, FENDER WASHER, FLAT WASHER & STAR KNOB TO HOLD STAND/TABLE

3"

45°

5"

#10 x 2½" FHWS (6 REQ'D)

SIDE VIEW

⅜" DIA HOLE THRU

2½"

1" (TYP)

1⅜"

MICRO-ADJUSTMENT JACK

22½"

½" WD x 1¼" DP DADO (TYP)

¾"

#10 x 1½" FHWS (6 REQ'D)

1½"

¾"

¾"

BACK VIEW

BASE
SUPPORT STAND

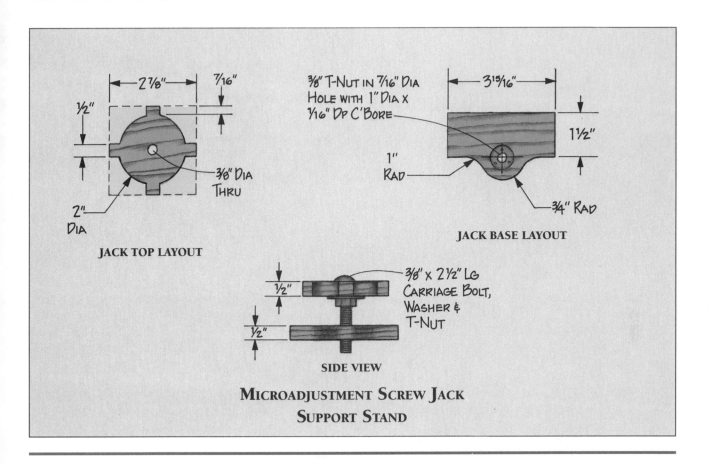

JACK TOP LAYOUT

JACK BASE LAYOUT

SIDE VIEW

MICROADJUSTMENT SCREW JACK
SUPPORT STAND

4 Cut the shapes and profiles. Miter the inside ends of the legs, the top corners of the support braces, and the bottom corners of the platform braces. Chamfer the top corner of the adjustment ledge. Using a band saw, scroll saw, or saber saw, cut the circular shape of the base and the profiles of the jack top and jack base. Sand the sawed edges.

5 Assemble the base. Finish sand all wooden surfaces. Glue the support, support sides, and support braces together. When the glue dries, fasten the base to this assembly with glue and flathead wood screws. Glue the feet to the square ends of the legs, then attach the legs to the base assembly with glue and flathead wood screws.

Press the T-nut into the counterbored hole in the jack base. Slide the jack base into the rabbets at the bottoms of the support stand sides. Mark the location of the T-nut (in the jack base) where it rests against the support stand base. Drill a 7/16-inch-diameter hole through the base and the front leg at this location, as shown in the *Base/Top View*.

Fasten the jack top to a 2½-inch-long carriage bolt with a flat washer and a hex nut. Thread the bolt through the T-nut in the jack base — the bottom end of the bolt should disappear into the 7/16-inch-diameter hole you just drilled in the support stand base. Store the microadjustment screw jack in this location when you're not using it.

6 Assemble the stand and table. Glue the platform, platform braces, post, and adjustment ledge together. Reinforce the glue joint between the braces and the post with flathead wood screws. Arrange the roller bearings in two staggered rows on top of the platform, as shown in the *Stand/Table/Top View*, and secure them with screws. Install the stand in the base and secure it with a 3-inch-long carriage bolt, fender washer, flat washer, and star knob.

Mark where the adjustment ledge rests against the top of the carriage bolt in the screw jack. Drill a ¼-inch-deep countersink in the bottom surface of the adjustment ledge at this location. This helps keep the stand steady when using the jack.

Glue the rails and stiles to the bottom of the table extension to help stiffen it. Attach the table to the platform with a piano hinge, positioning the extension so it's slightly below the tops of the roller

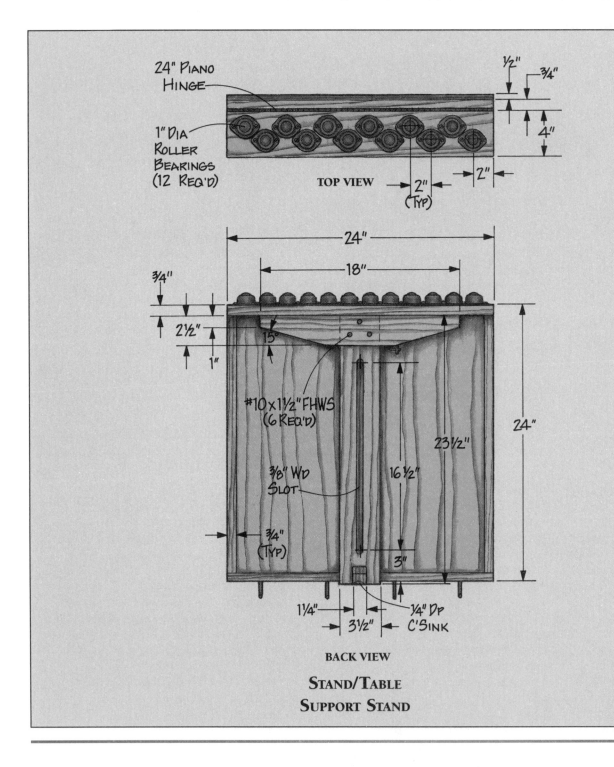

24" PIANO
HINGE

1" DIA
ROLLER
BEARINGS
(12 REQ'D)

TOP VIEW

½"
¾"
4"
2"
(TYP)
2"

¾"
2½"
1"
15°
24"
18"

#10 x 1½" FHWS
(6 REQ'D)

⅜" WD
SLOT

¾"
(TYP)

24"

23½"

16½"

3"

1¼"
3½"
¼" DP
C'SINK

BACK VIEW

**STAND/TABLE
SUPPORT STAND**

bearings when the extension is horizontal. Install a hook and eye under the table and the platform braces to keep the table vertical when it's not being used. Also install L-hooks to the outside rail of the table extension. The bottom surfaces of the hook shanks must be ¾ inch below the tabletop, as shown in the

L-Hook Detail, and the positions of the hooks must match the holes in the ledgers. **Note:** If necessary, bend the hooks slightly to adjust their positions.

7 **Finish the support stand.** Disassemble the stand, table, and base, removing all the hardware.

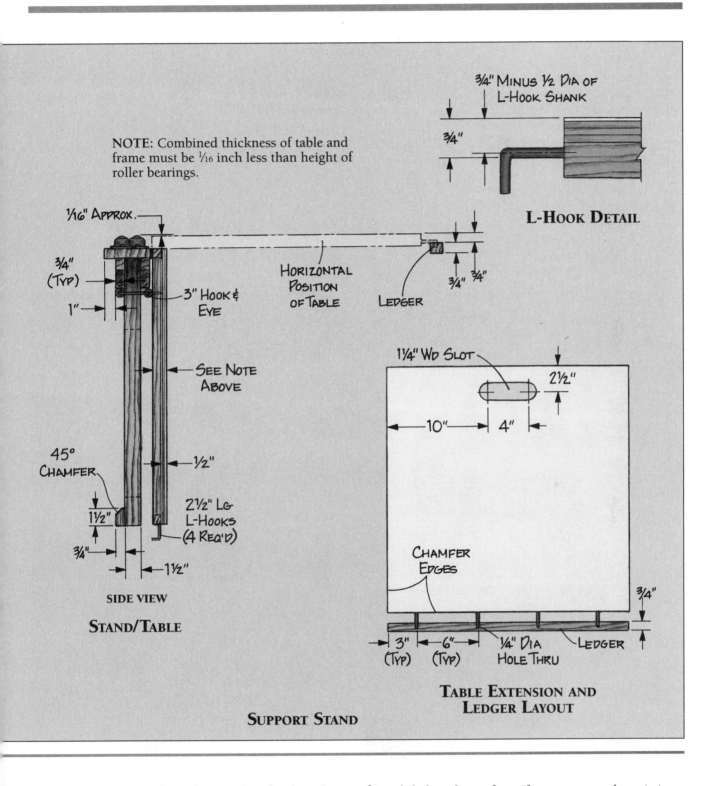

NOTE: Combined thickness of table and frame must be 1/16 inch less than height of roller bearings.

3/4" MINUS 1/2 DIA OF L-HOOK SHANK

3/4"

L-HOOK DETAIL

1/16" APPROX.

3/4" (TYP)

1"

3" HOOK & EYE

HORIZONTAL POSITION OF TABLE

LEDGER

3/4"   3/4"

SEE NOTE ABOVE

1 1/4" WD SLOT

2 1/2"

10"   4"

45° CHAMFER

1/2"

1 1/2"

3/4"

2 1/2" LG L-HOOKS (4 REQ'D)

1 1/2"

CHAMFER EDGES

3/4"

SIDE VIEW

STAND/TABLE

3" (TYP)   6" (TYP)

1/4" DIA HOLE THRU

LEDGER

SUPPORT STAND

TABLE EXTENSION AND LEDGER LAYOUT

Do any necessary sanding, then apply a finish. When the finish dries, reassemble the project.

8 **Install the ledgers.** Fasten the ledgers to the work surface of your power tools wherever you can use a table extension. Each ledger must be precisely

3/4 inch below the surface. If you can, use the existing holes in the tools to bolt or screw the ledgers in place. If that's not possible, drill the holes where you need them. **Note:** In some cases, you may have to modify the ledger or the table to fit the tool.

5. ADJUSTABLE-HEIGHT FENCE

A tall fence helps control wide boards while you cut or shape the edge — cutting a groove, drilling a series of holes, jointing, resawing, and so on. If the fence is too tall, however, it can hinder as much as it helps. An overly tall fence restricts access to the work and gets in the way of the machinery. This is especially true when resawing on the band saw — when the fence is taller than the board you're resawing, you can't position the upper blade guide properly.

Some craftsmen deal with this problem by keeping several fences of different heights on hand. But this takes up storage space and it still doesn't guarantee you'll have the height you need. This *adjustable-height fence* is a better solution. It consists of three rails held together with braces and guides. Loosen the machine screws that hold the parts together and you can quickly change the height of the fence from 6 inches (A) to 12 inches (B), or any height in between. When resawing, you can set the top of the fence just below the top edge of the board you're cutting — right where it should be (C).

Furthermore, you can attach this fixture to any power tool. Just clamp, screw, or bolt it to the existing fences.

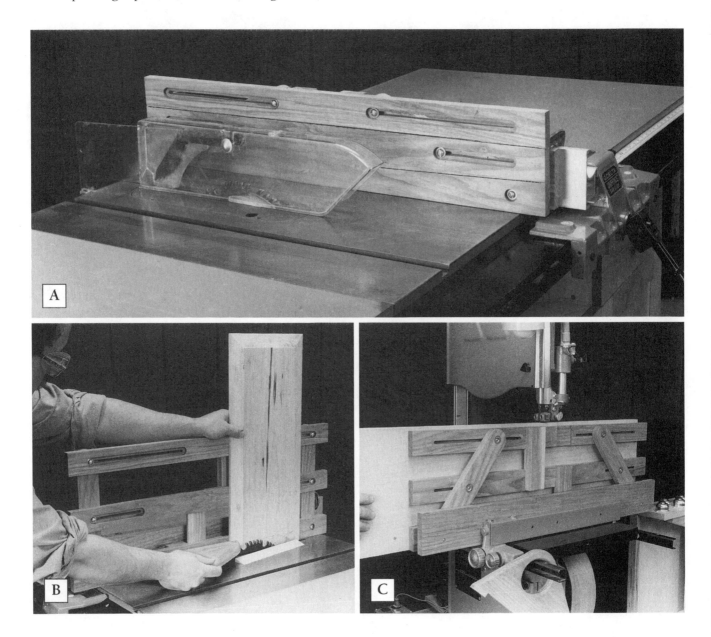

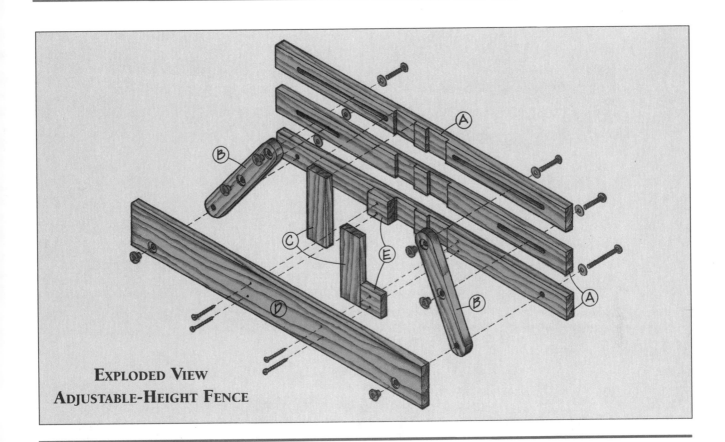

**EXPLODED VIEW
ADJUSTABLE-HEIGHT FENCE**

MATERIALS LIST (FINISHED DIMENSIONS)

Parts

A. Rails (3)   ¾" x 2" x 30"
B. Braces (2)   ¾" x 2" x 12"
C. Guides (2)   ¾" x 2" x 6"
D. Mounting
   board   ¾" x (variable)* x 30"
E. Spacers (2)   ¾" x 2" x 2"

Hardware

#8 x 1¼" Flathead wood screws
  (4)
¼" x 1¼" Roundhead machine
  screws (4)
¼" x 2" Roundhead machine
  screws (2)
³⁄₁₆" Flat washers (6)†
¼" T-nuts (6)

*Make this dimension equal to the height of the tallest fence to which you will attach this fixture. In most shops, this will either be the table saw fence or the router table fence.
†A ³⁄₁₆" washer fits a ¼" machine screw more closely than a ¼" washer.

PLAN OF PROCEDURE

1 Select the stock and cut the parts. To make this fixture, you need approximately 3 board feet of 4/4 (four-quarters) hardwood. Select clear, straight-grained stock and let it shop-dry for several weeks to stabilize. Then plane the stock to ¾ inch thick and cut the parts to size.

2 Drill the holes. Lay out the holes and slots on the rails, braces, and mounting board. Then drill these holes:

■ ⁵⁄₁₆-inch-diameter counterbored holes for T-nuts in the braces and mounting board, as shown in the *Back View* and the *Brace Layout*
■ ¼-inch-diameter counterbored holes in the bottom rail, as shown in the *Front View*
■ ¼-inch-diameter holes in the braces

3 Cut the slots and dadoes. Cut 2-inch-wide, ¼-inch-deep dadoes in the back face of the rails, as shown in the *Top View*. Rout ¼-inch-wide counter-

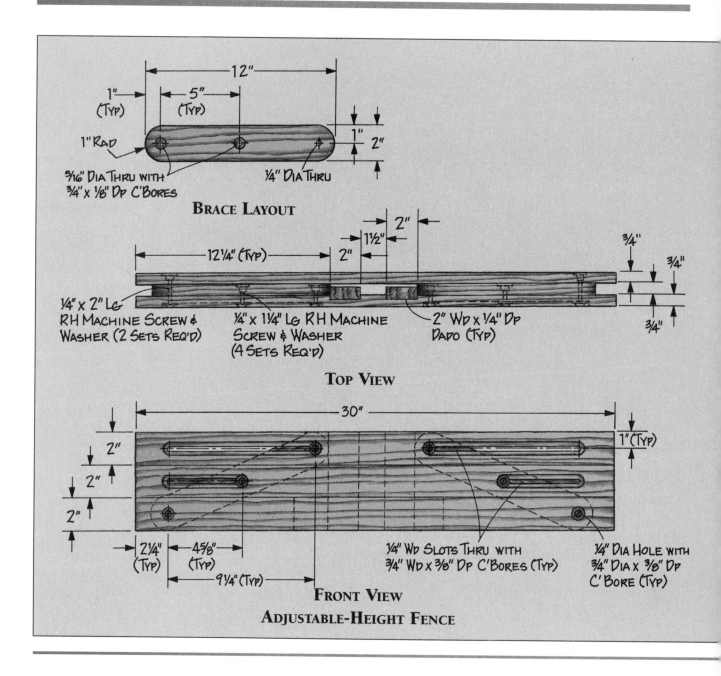

BRACE LAYOUT

12"

1" (TYP)

5" (TYP)

1" RAD

1"

2"

5/16" DIA THRU WITH 3/4" X 1/8" DP C'BORES

1/4" DIA THRU

TOP VIEW

12 1/4" (TYP)

2"

1 1/2"

2"

3/4"

3/4"

3/4"

1/4" X 2" LG RH MACHINE SCREW & WASHER (2 SETS REQ'D)

1/4" X 1 1/4" LG RH MACHINE SCREW & WASHER (4 SETS REQ'D)

2" WD X 1/4" DP DADO (TYP)

FRONT VIEW
ADJUSTABLE-HEIGHT FENCE

30"

2"

2"

2"

1" (TYP)

2 1/4" (TYP)

4 5/8" (TYP)

9 1/4" (TYP)

1/4" WD SLOTS THRU WITH 3/4" WD X 3/8" DP C'BORES (TYP)

1/4" DIA HOLE WITH 3/4" DIA X 3/8" DP C'BORE (TYP)

bored slots in the middle and top rails, as shown in the *Front View*. (Refer to "Holes, Counterbores, and Slots" on page 15 for instructions on making a counterbored slot.)

4 Assemble and finish the fence. Finish sand the parts. Lay the rails face down on your workbench, aligning the dadoes. Glue the spacers to the bottom rail beside the dadoes, as shown on the *Back View*. Also glue one guide in the right dado on the bottom rail and the other guide in the left dado on the top rail. When the glue dries, widen the other dadoes

slightly with a file so the guides will slide through them easily.

Install the T-nuts in the braces and mounting board. Fasten the mounting board to the spacers on the bottom rail with flathead wood screws. *Don't glue these parts together* — you may need to remove the mounting board from time to time. Attach the braces and remaining rails with roundhead machine screws and washers.

With the machine screws loose, the fence should extend and collapse easily. When you're satisfied it works properly, collapse the fence and tighten the

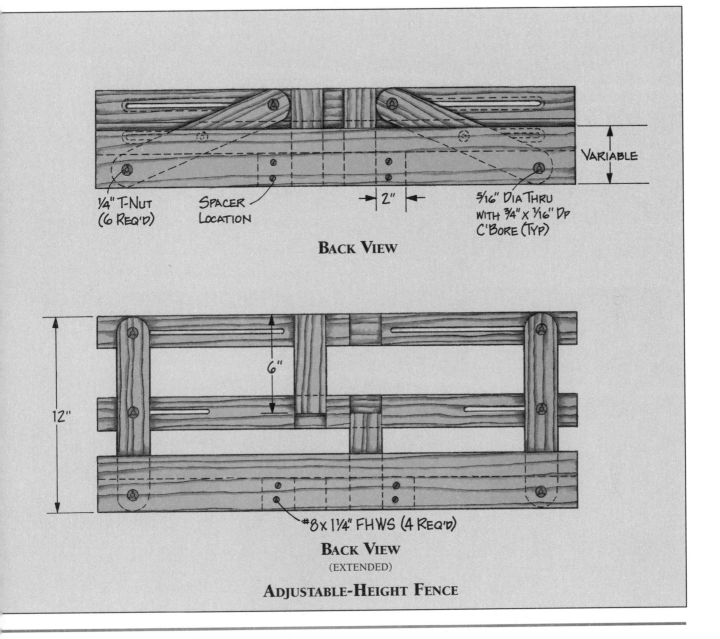

¼" T-Nut
(6 Req'd)

Spacer
Location

← 2" →

5/16" Dia Thru
with ¾" x 1/16" Dp
C'Bore (Typ)

Back View

Variable

12"

6"

#8 x 1¼" FHWS (4 Req'd)

Back View
(EXTENDED)

Adjustable-Height Fence

screws. Check that the heads of the screws are well below the surface of the rails, then joint the front face of the fence flat. Be careful not to remove too much stock — you don't want to nick the machine screws with the jointer knives.

Disassemble the fence and set the hardware aside. Apply a finish to all wooden parts. When the finish dries, reassemble the fence.

5 **Mount the fence on your power tools.** There are several simple ways to mount this fixture to your power tools:

■ Clamp the mounting board to the existing power tool fence.

■ Drive wood screws through the power tool fence and into the mounting board. (Many commercial power tool fences have predrilled holes to attach jigs and fixtures.)

■ Drill counterbored holes in the mounting board that correspond to the holes in the power tool fence. (The counterbores must be on the *inside* face.) Install T-nuts in the counterbored holes, then attach the mounting board to the fence with machine screws.

6. TENONING JIG

A tenoning jig holds a board vertically while you cut, shape, or rout its end. The jig is essential for cutting tenons, end laps, spline grooves, and similar operations. This particular jig has a cleat that hooks over a power tool fence and rides along it. If you want to use the jig with different power tools, remove the cleat and guide the jig along any fence or straightedge.

The backstop supports the work at any angle from 45 to 90 degrees to the worktable (*A* and *B*). Note that the work is supported *all the way to the worktable* no matter what angle the backstop is adjusted to. The adjustable backstops on other tenoning jigs end several inches above the worktable, leaving the work partially unsupported. To provide better support,

I developed a unique system of slots that allow the backstop to slide and pivot in such a way that the lower end remains in contact with the worktable (*C*).

I also installed two shop-made clamps to better secure the work in the jig. Many tenoning jigs rely on a single toggle clamp for this task, but in my experience, a toggle clamp just doesn't apply enough pressure to hold a piece securely. My clamps grip the piece firmly from both edges for trouble-free cutting. The forward clamp can be moved to several different positions, depending on the width of the work, the angle at which it's held, and where you need to apply pressure.

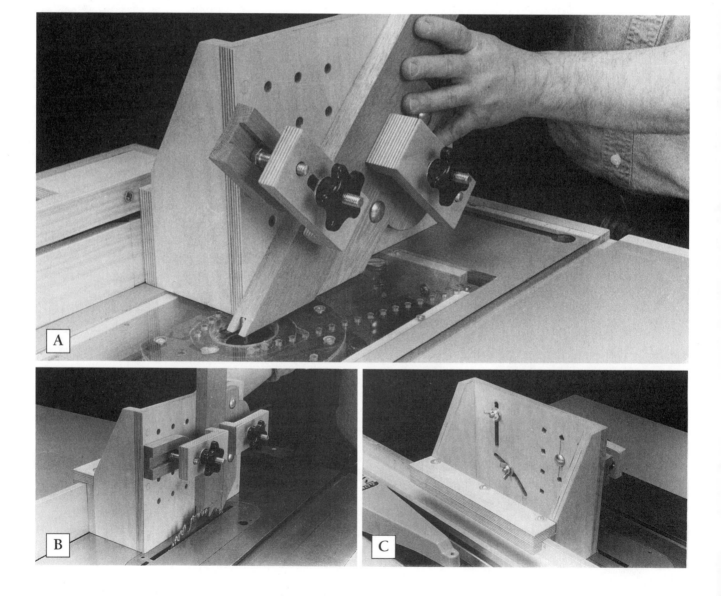

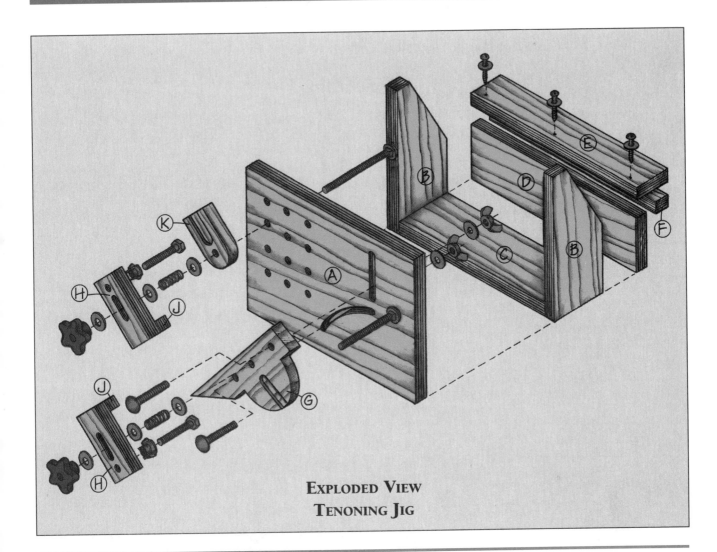

EXPLODED VIEW
TENONING JIG

MATERIALS LIST (FINISHED DIMENSIONS)

Parts

A. Face* $\frac{3}{4}'' \times 11''^{\dagger} \times 12''$
B. Sides (2)* $\frac{3}{4}'' \times 3\frac{5}{8}'' \times 9''$
C. Bottom* $\frac{3}{4}'' \times 3\frac{5}{8}'' \times 10\frac{1}{2}''$
D. Back* $\frac{3}{4}'' \times$ (variable)$^{\ddagger} \times 12''$
E. Rail* $\frac{3}{4}'' \times$ (variable)$^{\ddagger} \times 12''$
F. Cleat* $\frac{3}{4}'' \times \frac{3}{4}'' \times 12''$
G. Backstop $\frac{3}{4}'' \times 4'' \times 9''$
H. Clamps (2)* $\frac{3}{4}'' \times 2'' \times 4\frac{3}{4}''$
J. Clamp jaws (2)* $\frac{3}{4}'' \times \frac{3}{4}'' \times 2''$
K. Clamp base $\frac{3}{4}'' \times 2'' \times 4''$

Hardware

#8 x 1½" Flathead wood screws
  (16)
#10 x 2" Roundhead wood screws
  (3)
⅜" x 4½" Carriage bolt
⅜" x 3½" Carriage bolt
⅜" x 2" Carriage bolts (2)
⅜" x 2¼" Hex bolts (2)
⅜" Flat washers (8)
#10 Flat washers (3)
⅜" Wing nuts (2)
⅜" Star knobs (2)
⅜" T-nuts (2)
⅜" I.D. x 1½" Compression
  springs (2)

* *Make these parts from plywood.*
† *Cut this dimension to 9" after routing the slots.*
‡ *These dimensions depend on the height and width of the power tool fence.*

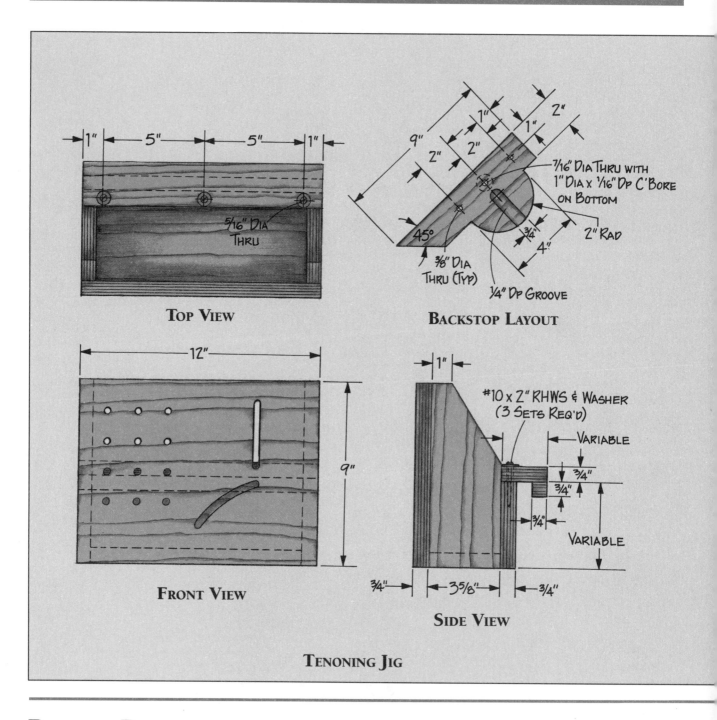

TOP VIEW

5/16" DIA THRU

BACKSTOP LAYOUT

7/16" DIA THRU WITH
1" DIA x 1/16" DP C'BORE
ON BOTTOM

2" RAD

3/8" DIA
THRU (TYP)

1/4" DP GROOVE

45°

FRONT VIEW

SIDE VIEW

#10 x 2" RHWS & WASHER
(3 SETS REQ'D)

VARIABLE

VARIABLE

TENONING JIG

PLAN OF PROCEDURE

1 **Select the stock and cut the parts.** To make
this tenoning jig, select a piece of ¾-inch plywood
approximately 12 inches by 36 inches (3 square feet),
along with some scraps of ¾-inch-thick hardwood.
Measure the height and the width of the fence on the
power tool where you will use the tenoning jig most
often. Then cut the parts to size, making the back as

tall as the fence, and the rail 1½ inches wider than the
fence. Miter the back corners of the sides, as shown in
the *Side View.*

2 **Drill the holes.** Lay out the hole locations on
the face, rail, backstop, clamps, and clamp base. Then
drill these holes:

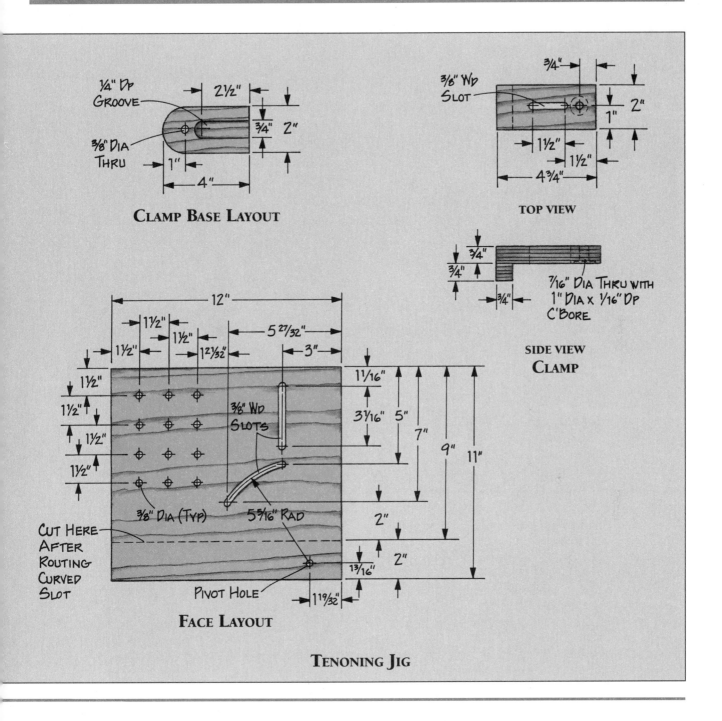

¼" Dp Groove

2½"

¾" 2"

⅜" Dia Thru

1"

4"

CLAMP BASE LAYOUT

⅜" Wd Slot

¾"

2"

1"

1½"

1½"

4¾"

TOP VIEW

¾"

¾"

¾"

⁷⁄₁₆" Dia Thru with 1" Dia x ¹⁄₁₆" Dp C'Bore

SIDE VIEW
CLAMP

12"

1½"

1½"

1½"

1½"

1²¹⁄₃₂"

5²⁷⁄₃₂"

3"

1½"

1½"

1½"

1½"

⅜" Wd Slots

1¹¹⁄₁₆"

3¹⁄₁₆" 5"

7"

9" 11"

⅜" Dia (Typ)

5⁵⁄₁₆" Rad

2"

2"

Cut Here After Routing Curved Slot

Pivot Hole

1³⁄₁₆"

2"

1¹⁹⁄₃₂"

FACE LAYOUT

TENONING JIG

■ ⁷⁄₁₆-inch-diameter counterbored holes in the clamps for the T-nuts, as shown in the *Clamp/Side View*

■ ⅜-inch-diameter holes — one with a counterbore — in the backstop, as shown in the *Backstop Layout*

■ ⅜-inch-diameter holes in the face — including the pivot hole — as shown in the *Face Layout*

■ ⅜-inch-diameter hole in the clamp base, as shown in the *Clamp Base Layout*

■ ⁵⁄₁₆-inch-diameter holes in the rail, as shown in the *Top View*

3 Rout the slots and grooves. Rout the ⅜-inch-wide slots in the face, as shown in the *Face Layout*.

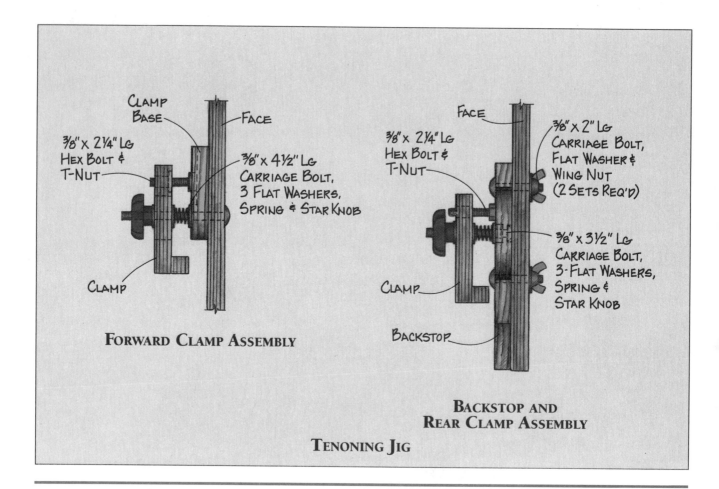

CLAMP
BASE

FACE

3/8" x 2¼" LG
HEX BOLT &
T-NUT

3/8" x 4½" LG
CARRIAGE BOLT,
3 FLAT WASHERS,
SPRING & STAR KNOB

CLAMP

FORWARD CLAMP ASSEMBLY

FACE

3/8" x 2¼" LG
HEX BOLT &
T-NUT

3/8" x 2" LG
CARRIAGE BOLT,
FLAT WASHER &
WING NUT
(2 SETS REQ'D)

3/8" x 3½" LG
CARRIAGE BOLT,
3-FLAT WASHERS,
SPRING &
STAR KNOB

CLAMP

BACKSTOP

**BACKSTOP AND
REAR CLAMP ASSEMBLY**

TENONING JIG

Use a router compass jig (shown in "Holes, Counterbores, and Slots" on page 15) to make the curved slot, swinging the compass jig around the pivot hole. When you've routed these slots, cut away the bottom edge of the face, making it 9 inches tall. Also rout the ⅜-inch-wide slots in the clamps and the ¾-inch-wide, ¼-inch-deep grooves in the backstop and the clamp base.

4 Cut the profiles. Using a band saw, scroll saw, or saber saw, cut the profiles of the backstop and clamp base. Sand the sawed edges.

5 Assemble and finish the tenoning jig. Finish sand the parts. Assemble the face, sides, bottom, and back to make a box. Glue the parts together, reinforcing the joints with flathead wood screws. Also glue the cleat to the rail. When the glue dries, attach the rail to the back with roundhead wood screws and washers.

Assemble the backstop and clamps and attach them to the face of the tenoning jig with bolts, washers, wing nuts, springs, and star knobs, as shown in the *Forward Clamp Assembly* and the *Backstop and Rear Clamp Assembly*. Loosen the wing nuts and test the action of the backstop — it should pivot from 90 degrees to 45 degrees off horizontal. As it does so, the mitered tip of the backstop should remain even with the bottom edge of the face.

When you're satisfied the tenoning jig works properly, disassemble it and set the hardware aside. Apply a finish to all wooden surfaces.

6 Adjust the rail. When the finish dries, reassemble the jig. Place it against the power tool fence, hooking the cleat over the fence top. Loosen the roundhead wood screws and adjust the position of the rail so the cleat holds the jig snug against the fence, then tighten the screws again. (The holes in the rail are slightly larger than the screws, letting you move the rail a fraction of an inch.) When the rail is properly adjusted, the jig should remain flat against the fence it travels along, but it shouldn't bind or be difficult to push.

7. SLIDING CUTOFF TABLE

The Achilles heel of almost every table saw is that, as it comes from the factory, it's a marginal tool for making crosscuts. Unless the manufacturer provides something better than the usual miter gauge, you have to make or purchase some kind of cutoff accessory to get the accuracy you need. My preference is a sliding table. It's large enough to handle big workpieces but light enough that you can remove it from the table saw and store it easily when you don't need it.

This particular sliding table travels back and forth in the left miter gauge slot on any table saw. The backstop is 30 inches long and extends to 48 inches for superlong cutoffs (A). Built-in scales help you measure the work as you cut it, and a stop lets you make duplicate cuts. The stop is microadjustable and stores on the rear of the backstop when you're not using it (B).

You can also use the sliding table to cut miters by angling the backstop (C). I designed this backstop to rotate in both directions (D), enabling you to make compound miters as well as simple miters. When it's mounted over the back pivot hole at the back of the table, it will swing 70 degrees to the right. Move it to the forward pivot hole, and you can swing it 45 degrees to the left. That's a range of 115 degrees! — quite a few more than most sliding tables offer.

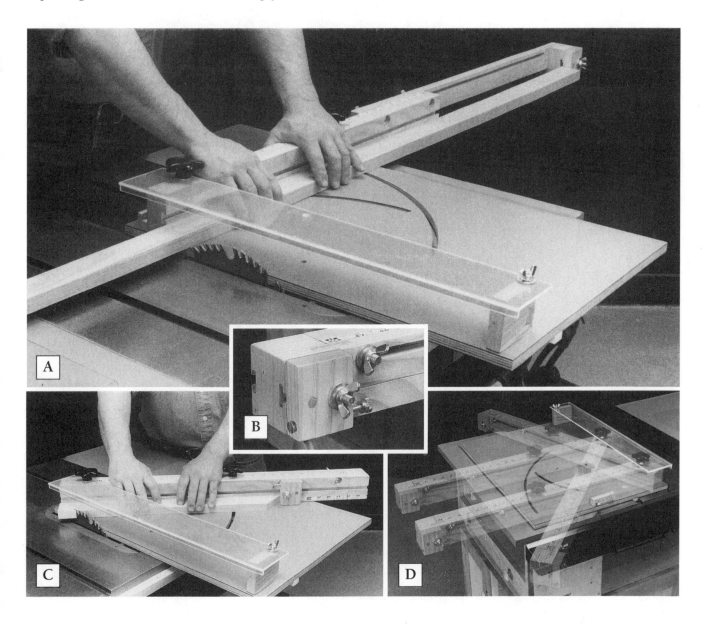

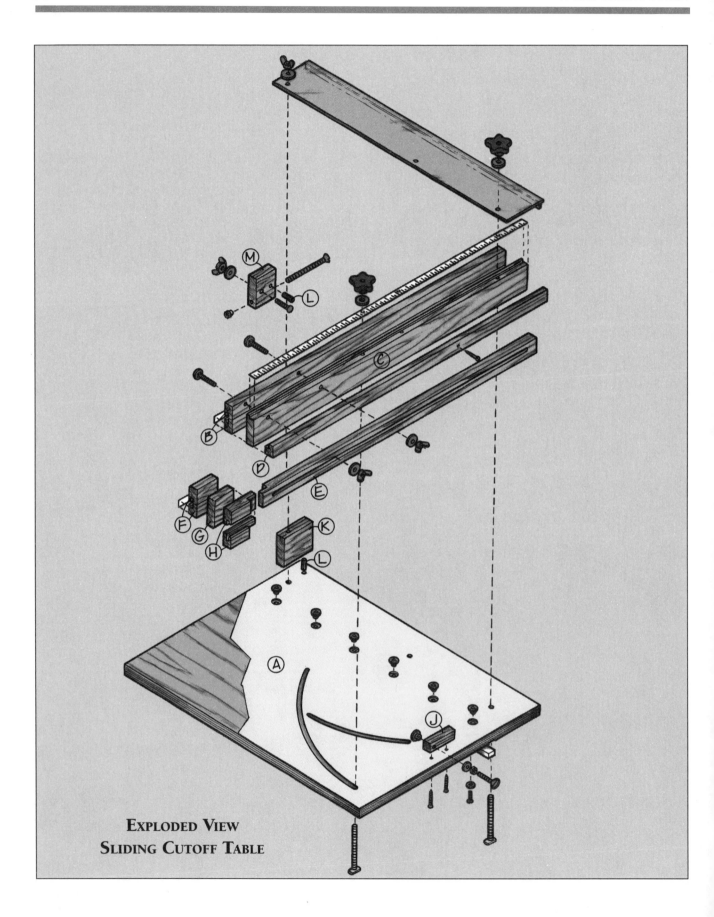

**EXPLODED VIEW
SLIDING CUTOFF TABLE**

MATERIALS LIST (FINISHED DIMENSIONS)

Parts

A. Sliding table* $\frac{1}{2}$" x 18" x 24"
B. Backstop top/bottom
   faces (2) $\frac{3}{4}$" x 1$\frac{1}{4}$" x 28"
C. Backstop
   center $\frac{3}{4}$" x 2$\frac{1}{2}$" x 28"
D. Backstop back $\frac{3}{4}$" x 1" x 28"
E. Backstop
   extension $\frac{3}{4}$" x 1$\frac{7}{8}$" x 28"
F. Extension top/bottom
   faces (2) $\frac{3}{4}$" x 1$\frac{1}{4}$" x 2"
G. Extension
   center $\frac{3}{4}$" x 2$\frac{1}{2}$" x 2"
H. Extension top/bottom
   backs (2) $\frac{3}{4}$" x 1$\frac{1}{4}$" x 2$\frac{3}{4}$"
J. Adjustment
   block $\frac{3}{4}$" x $\frac{3}{4}$" x 3"
K. Guard support $\frac{3}{4}$" x 2$\frac{1}{2}$" x 3"
L. Dowels (2) $\frac{5}{16}$" dia. x 1"
M. Stop $\frac{3}{4}$" x 2$\frac{1}{2}$" x 2"

Hardware

#6 x 1" Flathead wood screws (3)
$\frac{5}{16}$" x 3$\frac{1}{2}$" Flange bolts (2)
$\frac{5}{16}$" x 3$\frac{1}{2}$" Carriage bolt
$\frac{5}{16}$" x 3" Carriage bolts (2)
$\frac{5}{16}$" x 1$\frac{1}{2}$" Carriage bolt
#10–32 x 3" Flathead machine
   screw
#10 x $\frac{3}{4}$" Roundhead machine
   screws (6)
#10 x 1" Thumbscrew
$\frac{5}{16}$" Flat washers (6)
#10 Flat washers (7)
$\frac{5}{16}$" Wing nuts (4)
#10 Brad-hole T-nuts (7)
#10 Hex nut
#10 Knurled knob
$\frac{5}{16}$" Star knobs (2)
$\frac{1}{8}$" Orange acrylic plastic
   (4" x 24" sheet)

$\frac{3}{8}$" UHMW plastic ($\frac{3}{4}$" x 24" strip)
   for guide bar
$\frac{1}{2}$" x 48" Right-to-left self-stick
   rules (2)
Plastic laminate
   (25" x 39" sheet — optional)

Make this part from European birch plywood.

PLAN OF PROCEDURE

1 Select the stock and cut the parts. To make this sliding table, you need approximately 3 board feet of 4/4 (four-quarters) hardwood and a sheet of $\frac{1}{2}$-inch European birch plywood at least 2 feet square. **Note:** The hardwood stock for the backstop parts must be straight and clear. Plane the 4/4 stock to $\frac{3}{4}$ inch thick, and cut all the parts to size except the sliding table, backstop faces, extension faces, and extension backs. For the sliding table, trim the plywood sheet to 19 inches wide by 24 inches long. For the remaining parts, cut two boards 1$\frac{1}{4}$ inches wide by 36 inches long.

2 Cut the joinery for the backstop and extension. Cut or rout the rabbets, grooves, and slots on these parts:

■ $\frac{3}{8}$-inch-wide, $\frac{3}{8}$-inch-deep rabbets in the edges of the backstop back and the backstop extension, as shown in the *Backstop/End View* and *Backstop Extension/Back View*

■ $\frac{5}{16}$-inch-wide slot in the backstop extension, as shown in the *Backstop Extension/Face View*

■ $\frac{3}{16}$-inch-wide, $\frac{3}{8}$-inch-deep groove in the edge of the two 36-inch-long boards, as shown in the *Backstop/End View* detail.

3 Make the faces. Cut one side of the groove in the 36-inch-long boards short. Glue the boards edge to edge to make a single piece 2$\frac{1}{2}$ inches wide with a T-slot in the center. Let the glue dry, then cut the backstop face, extension face, and extension back from this stock.

4 Assemble the backstop and backstop extension. Glue the backstop face, backstop center, and backstop back together to make the backstop. Cut $\frac{3}{4}$-inch-wide, $\frac{3}{8}$-inch-deep rabbets in the adjoining ends of the backstop extension and the extension back, as shown in the *Backstop Extension/Top View*. Glue the backstop extension, extension face, extension center, and extension back together. When the glue dries, use a dovetail saw or a coping saw to notch the corner of the extension back, as shown in the *Backstop Extension/Back View*.

5 Drill the backstop assembly. Drill the $\frac{5}{16}$-inch-diameter counterbored holes through the backstop horizontally, as shown in the *Backstop/Face View*, and the $\frac{5}{16}$-inch-diameter holes through the backstop vertically, as shown in the *Backstop/Top View*.

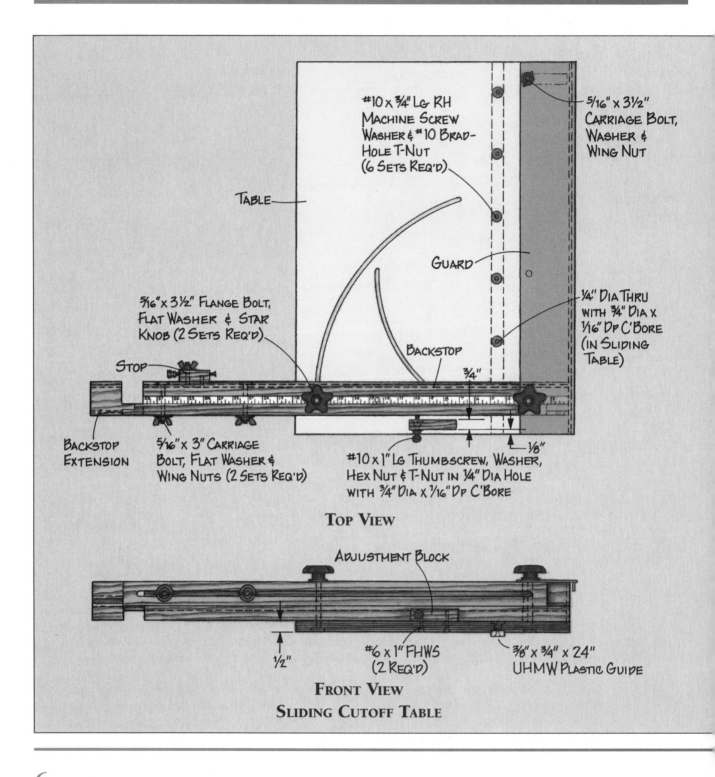

#10 x ¾" Lg RH Machine Screw Washer & #10 Brad- Hole T-Nut (6 Sets Req'd)

5/16" x 3½" Carriage Bolt, Washer & Wing Nut

Table

Guard

5/16" x 3½" Flange Bolt, Flat Washer & Star Knob (2 Sets Req'd)

¼" Dia Thru with ¾" Dia x 1/16" Dp C'Bore (in Sliding Table)

Backstop

¾"

Stop

1/8"

Backstop Extension

5/16" x 3" Carriage Bolt, Flat Washer & Wing Nuts (2 Sets Req'd)

#10 x 1" Lg Thumbscrew, Washer, Hex Nut & T-Nut in ¼" Dia Hole with ¾" Dia x 1/16" Dp C'Bore

TOP VIEW

Adjustment Block

½"

#6 x 1" FHWS (2 Req'd)

3/8" x ¾" x 24" UHMW Plastic Guide

FRONT VIEW
SLIDING CUTOFF TABLE

6 **Install the rules.** Secure the backstop extension to the backstop with carriage bolts, washers, and wing nuts. Make sure the heads of the bolts are well below the wood surface, then joint the faces of the backstop and the extension perfectly flat. Cut ½-inch-wide, 1/32-inch-deep rabbets for the rules in the extension face and backstop face, along the bottom edges. Remove the extension and the hardware from the backstop and cut a ½-inch-wide, 1/32-inch-deep groove in the top of the backstop center.

Adhere the rules in these recesses, as shown in the *Backstop/Face View, Backstop/Top View,* and *Backstop*

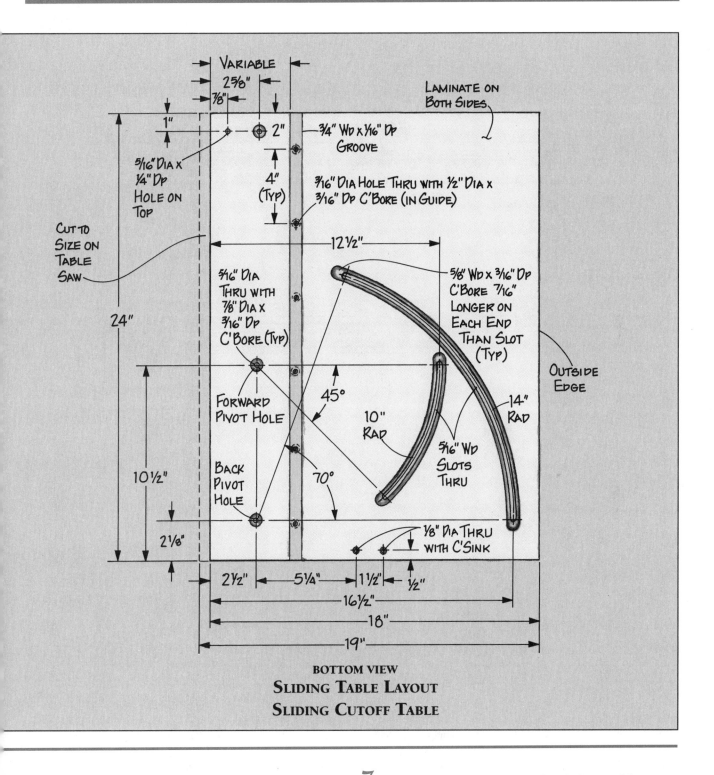

BOTTOM VIEW
SLIDING TABLE LAYOUT
SLIDING CUTOFF TABLE

Extension/Face View. Note that the rules on the backstop face and extension face are installed upside down so you can read them easily as you lean over the backstop. Drill 5/16-inch-diameter holes in the rule on the backstop center where it covers the holes you have already made.

7 Attach the guide bar to the sliding table. To make the table more durable, cover both faces of the plywood with plastic laminate. Measure the distance from the saw blade to the left miter gauge slot on your table saw. Lay out the location of the UHMW guide bar and the mounting holes on the bottom surface of

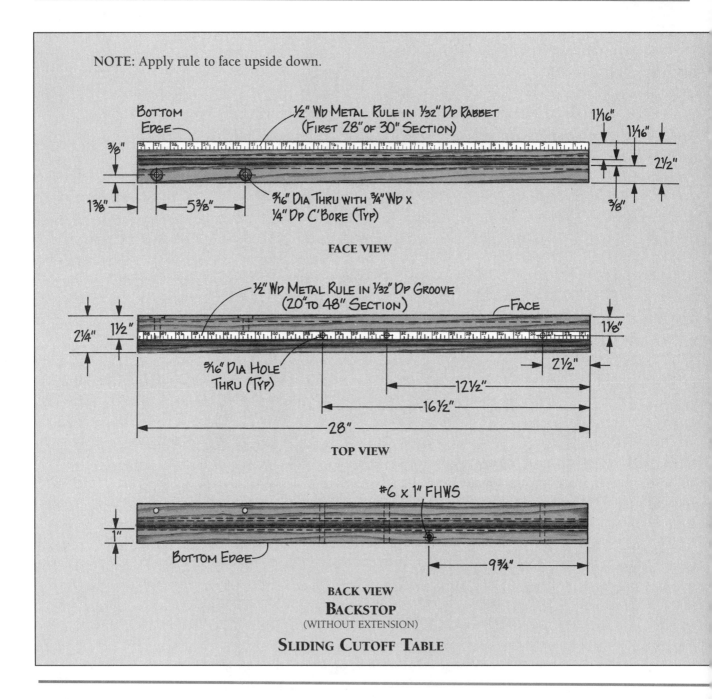

NOTE: Apply rule to face upside down.

BOTTOM EDGE

½" WD METAL RULE IN ⅟32" DP RABBET
(FIRST 28" OF 30" SECTION)

1⅟16"
1⅟16"
2½"

3/8"

1⅜"   5⅜"

⁵⁄16" DIA THRU WITH ¾" WD x
¼" DP C'BORE (TYP)

3/8"

FACE VIEW

½" WD METAL RULE IN ⅟32" DP GROOVE
(20" TO 48" SECTION)

FACE

2¼" 1½"

1⅛"

⁵⁄16" DIA HOLE
THRU (TYP)

2½"

12½"

16½"

28"

TOP VIEW

#6 x 1" FHWS

1"

BOTTOM EDGE

9¾"

BACK VIEW
BACKSTOP
(WITHOUT EXTENSION)
SLIDING CUTOFF TABLE

the table, positioning the guide bar *1 inch farther* from the inside edge of the table than the saw blade is from the slot.

Cut a ¾-inch-wide, ⁄16-inch-deep groove in the bottom surface of the table to hold the guide. Drill ³⁄16-inch-diameter counterbored holes in the guide, as shown in the *Sliding Table Layout/Bottom View*. Use the guide to mark the locations of the ¼-inch-diameter counterbored mounting holes on the table, then drill them, as shown in the *Top View*.

Attach the guide to the table with machine screws, washers, and T-nuts. Make sure the assembly slides back and forth easily in the left miter gauge slot, then turn on the table saw and trim the inside edge of the sliding table. When trimmed to its final size, the table should be approximately 18 inches wide and 24 inches long.

8 Make the guard. Cut the orange plastic into two 24-inch-long strips, one 3½ inches wide and the other

NOTE: Apply rule to face upside down.

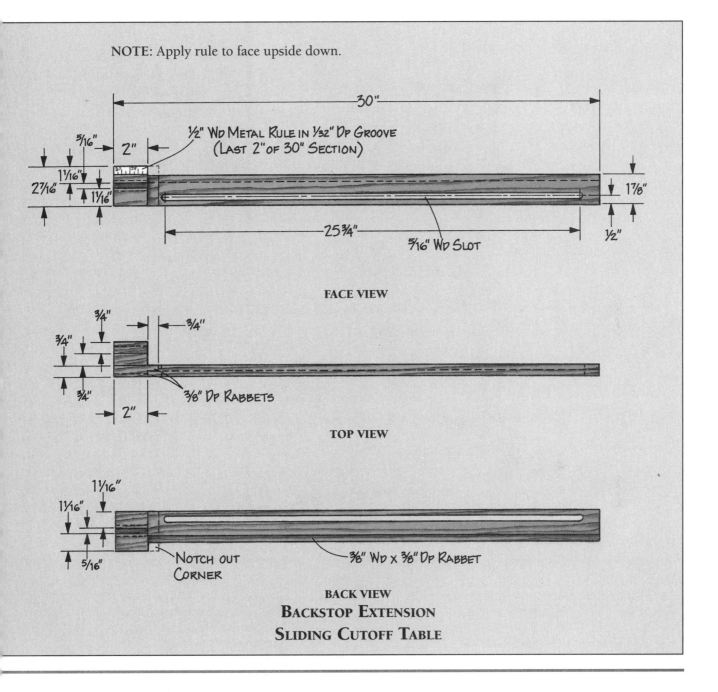

FACE VIEW

TOP VIEW

BACK VIEW
BACKSTOP EXTENSION
SLIDING CUTOFF TABLE

⅜ inch wide. Using acrylic cement (available from any plastics supplier), glue the strips together, as shown in the *Guard/End View.*

9 Drill the remaining holes. Lay out the locations of the remaining holes on the sliding table, including the forward and back pivot holes. Also lay out the holes in the stop, guard, guard support, and adjustment block. Then drill the holes you've marked:

■ ⁵⁄₁₆-inch-diameter holes in the sliding table, three

with counterbores and one just ¼ inch deep, as shown in the *Sliding Table Layout/Bottom View*

■ ⁵⁄₁₆-inch-diameter holes (one counterbored) in the stop, as shown in the *Stop/Front View* and *Stop/End View*

■ ⁵⁄₁₆-inch-diameter holes in the guard support, one through and one ¾ inch deep, as shown in the *Guard Support/Front View*

■ ⁵⁄₁₆-inch-diameter holes through the guard, as shown in the *Guard/Top View*

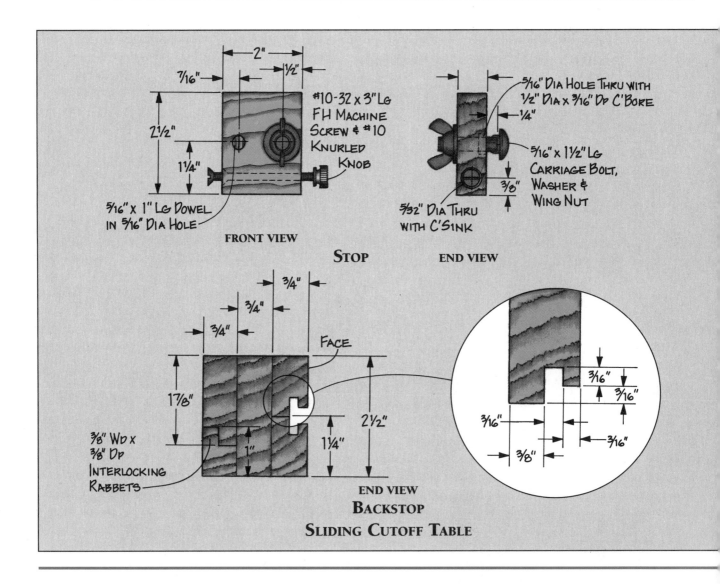

2"

7/16"   1/2"

2½"

1¼"

#10-32 x 3"LG
FH MACHINE
SCREW & #10
KNURLED
KNOB

5/16" x 1" LG DOWEL
IN 5/16" DIA HOLE

FRONT VIEW

5/16" DIA HOLE THRU WITH
½" DIA x 3/16" DP C'BORE
¼"

5/16" x 1½" LG
CARRIAGE BOLT,
WASHER &
WING NUT
3/8"

5/32" DIA THRU
WITH C'SINK

END VIEW

STOP

3/4"

3/4"

3/4"

FACE

1⅞"

3/8" WD x
3/8" DP
INTERLOCKING
RABBETS

1"

2½"

1¼"

3/16"

3/16"

3/16"

3/8"

3/16"

3/8"

END VIEW
BACKSTOP
SLIDING CUTOFF TABLE

■ ¼-inch-diameter counterbored hole in the adjustment block, as shown in the *Adjustment Block Layout*

■ 5/32-inch-diameter countersunk hole through the stop

■ ⅛-inch-diameter countersunk holes in the sliding table

■ ⅛-inch-diameter, ½-inch-deep holes in the adjustment block

Using a 10–32 tap, cut threads in the 5/32-inch-diameter hole in the stop.

10 **Cut the curved slots.** Use a router compass jig to rout the curved counterbored slots in the bottom of the table. (Refer to "Holes, Counterbores, and Slots" on page 15.) Swing the compass around the back pivot hole to make the 14-inch-radius slot, and

around the forward pivot hole to make the 10-inch-radius slot. Note that the counterbores on both slots are slightly longer than the slots themselves — this accommodates the flanges on the flange bolts.

11 **Assemble the sliding table.** Glue the dowels in the stop and the guard support, as shown in the *Stop/Front View* and *Guard Support/Front View*. Install a T-nut, thumbscrew, washer, and hex nut in the adjustment block, then fasten the block to the sliding table with flathead wood screws. Assemble the backstop and the extension. Install the hardware in the stop and mount the stop on the extension. Insert flange bolts through the 14-inch-radius slot and the back pivot hole, then mount the backstop over them. Put a carriage bolt through the mounting hole in the front of the table and place the guard support over it. Put

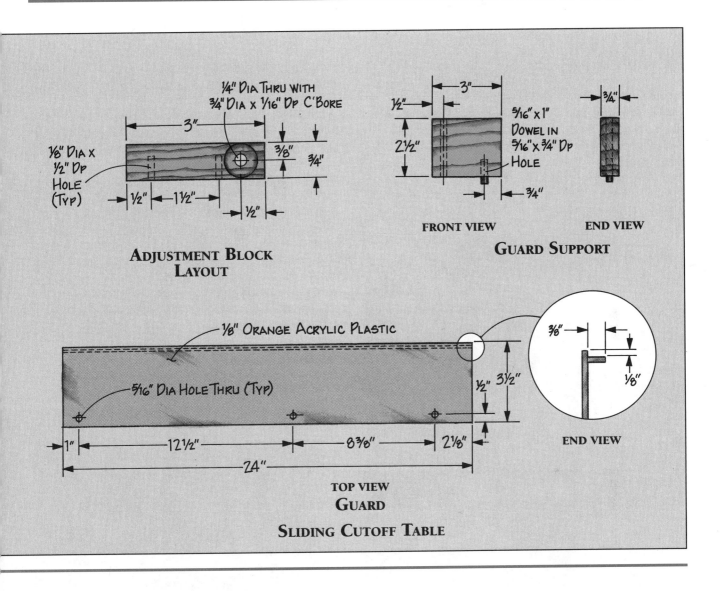

¼" DIA THRU WITH
¾" DIA X 1/16" DP C'BORE

⅛" DIA X
½" DP
HOLE
(TYP)

3"

3/8"

¾"

½" 1½"

½"

**ADJUSTMENT BLOCK
LAYOUT**

½"

3"

¾"

2½"

5/16" X 1"
DOWEL IN
5/16" X ¾" DP
HOLE

¾"

FRONT VIEW

END VIEW

GUARD SUPPORT

⅛" ORANGE ACRYLIC PLASTIC

3/8"

5/16" DIA HOLE THRU (TYP)

½" 3½"

⅛"

END VIEW

1"

12½"

8 3/8"

2⅛"

24"

**TOP VIEW
GUARD**

SLIDING CUTOFF TABLE

the guard in place over the carriage bolt and the right flange bolt, then secure all the parts with washers, star knobs, and wing nuts.

Check that the backstop moves easily in the 14-inch-radius slot and mark the backstop where the thumbscrew in the adjustment block touches it. Remove the backstop from the table and install a flat-head wood screw where you've marked it — the head of the screw should be flush with the wood surface. Also mount the backstop over the forward pivot hole and check its motion in the 10-inch-radius slot.

12 **Finish and adjust the sliding table.** When you're satisfied the backstop works properly, disassemble the sliding table and set the hardware aside. Do any necessary sanding and apply a finish to all wooden parts. When the finish dries, reassemble the

table. As you replace the hardware, glue the knurled knob permanently to the back end of the machine screw in the stop with cyanoacrylate cement (such as Super Glue). Or, mash the threads slightly before turning the knob onto the screw.

Place the sliding table on the table saw and adjust the thumbscrew so the backstop is precisely 90 degrees from the saw blade. Attach the stop to the extension face so the right edges are flush. Slide the extension sideways until the right edge of the stop block is exactly 30 inches from the left-beveled points of the saw teeth. Make an indexing mark on the top edge of the extension corresponding to the 30-inch mark on the rule on top of the backstop. When using this mark, remember that it indicates the distance from the saw blade to the right edge of the extension face.

8. LIFT-TOP ROUTER TABLE

A router table turns your portable router into a stationary power tool, doubling its usefulness. For many routing operations, it's easier and safer to pass the work over the router than it is to pass the router over the work (A). Despite that, standard router tables are somewhat awkward to use. With the router buried beneath the work surface, you have to stoop or kneel to change the bits or adjust the depth of cut. You may have to get up and down dozens of times during a single routing session.

To save my knees and back, I developed this lift-top router table. The top swings up like the lid of a chest, raising the router and holding it at a comfortable angle while you change bits or make adjustments *standing straight up*. You don't have to remove the fence or break down the setups on the work surface to raise the table — just release two draw catches on the front legs and lift up. A brace automatically swings down to hold the table in the raised position (B).

My lift-top router table includes several additional user-friendly features:

■ The fence includes a built-in dust pickup, movable faces to adjust the router bit opening, and a T-slot to attach stops and other fixtures.

■ All the measuring tools you need are close at hand. Rules on the detachable guard measure the depth of cut (C), and centering rules inlaid in the work surface help to position the fence (D).

■ There's plenty of storage. Pull-out brackets in the front of the stand hold the fence when it's not needed, and lift-out shelves and trays hold router bits, wrenches, and other accessories (E).

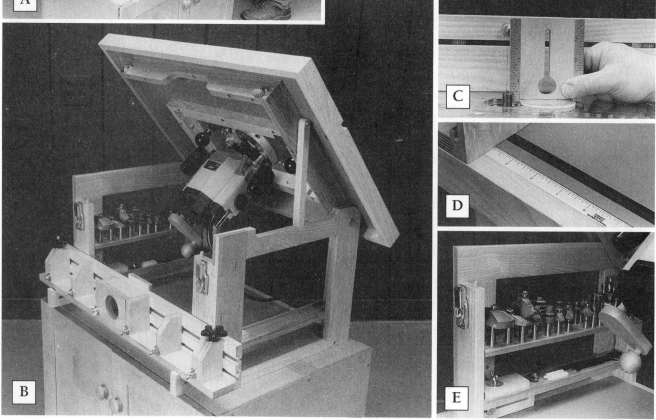

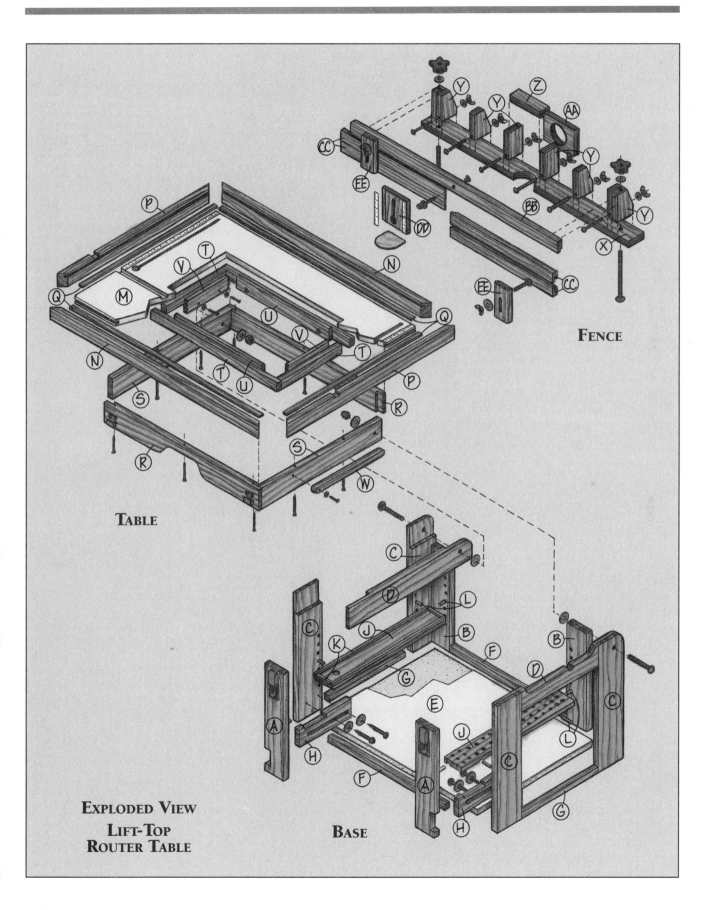

FENCE

TABLE

EXPLODED VIEW
LIFT-TOP
ROUTER TABLE

BASE

MATERIALS LIST (FINISHED DIMENSIONS)

Parts

Base

A. Front legs
(2)   ¾″ x 2¾″ x 12¾″
B. Back legs (2)   ¾″ x 2¾″ x 12″
C. Side legs (4) ¾″ x 3½″ x 15¼″
D. Rails (2)   ¾″ x 2½″ x 18″
E. Base*   ¾″ x 16½″ x 22½″
F. Front/back
trim (2)   ¾″ x ¾″ x 17″
G. Side trim (2)   ¾″ x ¾″ x 11″
H. Fence brackets
(2)   ¾″ x 2″ x 7½″
J. Tray/shelf
(2–4)   ½″ x 2¾″ x 16⅜″
K. Tray trim
(total, per tray) ¼″ x ¼″ x 40″
L. Shelving support dowels
(8–16)   ¼″ dia. x 1″

Table

M. Table*   ¾″ x 20½″ x 28½″
N. Front/back
banding (2)   ¾″ x 1¾″ x 30″
P. Side banding
(2)   ¾″ x 1¾″ x 22″
Q. Splines† (total) ¼″ x ¾″ x 108″
R. Front/back
aprons (2)   ¾″ x 2½″ x 22⅜″
S. Side aprons
(2)   ¾″ x 2½″ x 17¼″
T. Stiffeners
(total)   ¾″ x 1″ x (variable)‡
U. Front/back ledgers
(2)   ½″ x 1¼″ x (variable)‡
V. Side ledgers
(2)   ½″ x 1¼″ x (variable)‡
W. Brace   ¾″ x ¾″ x 9⅞″

Fence

X. Fence base†   ¾″ x 2¼″ x 30″
Y. Fence braces
(8)†   ¾″ x 2¼″ x 3¼″
Z. Dust pickup
top†   ¾″ x 2¼″ x 4½″
AA. Dust pickup
back†   ¾″ x 2½″ x 4½″
BB. Fixed face   ¾″ x 1³⁄₁₆″ x 30″
CC. Movable
faces (4)   ¾″ x 1¼″ x 15″
DD. Guard mount   ½″ x 3½″ x 4″
EE. Stops (2)   ¾″ x 2″ x 4″

Hardware

Base

#12 x 1½″ Roundhead wood
screws (4)
⁵⁄₁₆″ x 2¼″ Carriage bolts (2)
⁵⁄₁₆″ Flat washers (2)
¼″ Flat washers (4)
⁵⁄₁₆″ Stop nuts (2)
2½″ Draw catches and mounting
screws (2)
Plastic laminate (18″ x 24″ sheet –
optional)

Table

#12 x 1½″ Roundhead wood
screws (11)
#12 x 1″ Roundhead wood screws
(8)
#8 x 1½″ Flathead wood screws
(8)
#6 x 1″ Flathead wood screws
(4–6)

¼″ Flat washers (9)
⅜″ Clear acrylic plastic (for
mounting plate§)
½″ x 24″ Self-stick centering rules
(2)
Plastic laminate
(22″ x 30″ sheet — optional)

Fence

#6 x 1″ Flathead wood screws (2)
⅜″ x 5½″ Carriage bolts (2)
⁵⁄₁₆″ x 3″ Carriage bolts (6)
⁵⁄₁₆″ x 1½″ Carriage bolts (2)
¼″ x 1″ Thumbscrew
⅜″ Flat washers (2)
⁵⁄₁₆″ Flat washers (6)
¼″ Flat washer
⅜″ Star knobs (2)
⁵⁄₁₆″ Wing nuts (6)
¼″ Hex nut
⅛″ Orange acrylic plastic (3″ x 3″
piece for guard)
½″ x 4″ Rules (2, in ¹⁄₃₂″ and ¹⁄₆₄″
increments)

*Make these parts from medium-density
fiberboard (MDF).
†Make these parts from plywood.
‡These dimensions depend on the size of
the mounting plate.
§Adjust the length and width of the
mounting plate to fit your router.

PLAN OF PROCEDURE

1 Select the stock and cut the parts. To make
this router table, you need about 12 board feet of 4/4
(four-quarters) hardwood, a 2-foot by 4-foot sheet of
medium-density fiberboard (MDF), some scraps of ¼-
inch and ¾-inch plywood, and an 18-inch length of
¼-inch-diameter dowel stock. Cut the base and the
table to size from MDF and cover them with plastic
laminate. (You can also use laminate-covered sink
cutouts for these parts. Sink cutouts are available at
many lumberyards and building supply outlets.)

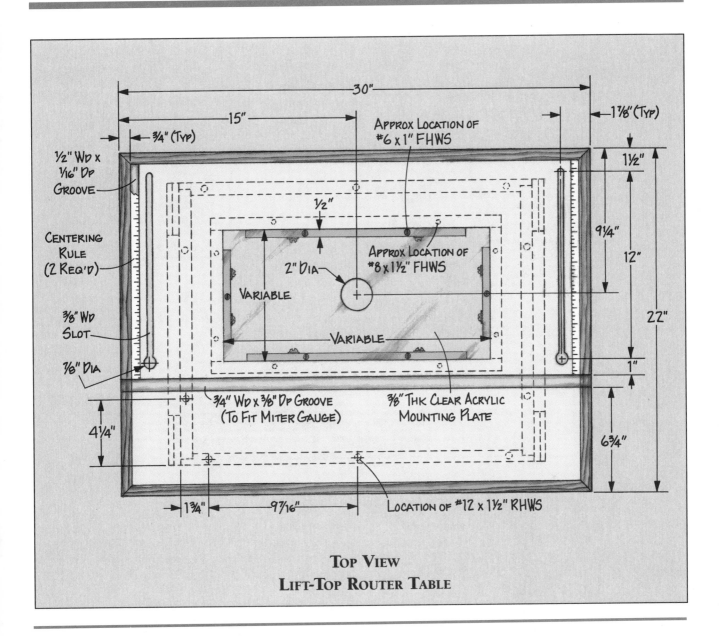

TOP VIEW
LIFT-TOP ROUTER TABLE

Plane the 4/4 stock to ¾ inch thick and cut the base parts to size, except for the base trim, shelves, trays, and tray trim. Decide how many shelves and trays you need for storage, then plane a small amount of ¾-inch-thick stock to ½ and ¼ inch thick — enough to make shelf and tray parts. Cut these parts to size.

Do not cut the table or the fence parts yet. This router table is easier to build if you divide it into three smaller projects — base, table, and fence.

MAKING THE BASE

2 Cut the joinery in the base parts. Cut the ⅜-inch-deep end laps in the top ends of the side legs

and both ends of the rails, as shown in the *Front View* and *Right Rail Layout/Top View*. Also rout the ¼-inch-wide slots in the fence brackets, as shown in the *Fence Bracket Layout*.

3 Drill the holes in the base parts. Lay out the ¼-inch-diameter, ½-inch-deep shelving support holes in the legs, as shown in the *Front View* and *Side View*, then drill them. Plan how you will arrange your router bits on the shelves, then drill ⅜-inch-deep holes in the top surfaces, sized to hold the bit shanks. Clamp the shelves and trays together, bottom to bottom, and drill ⁵/₁₆-inch-diameter, ¾-inch-deep holes in the edges where the parts meet. This will

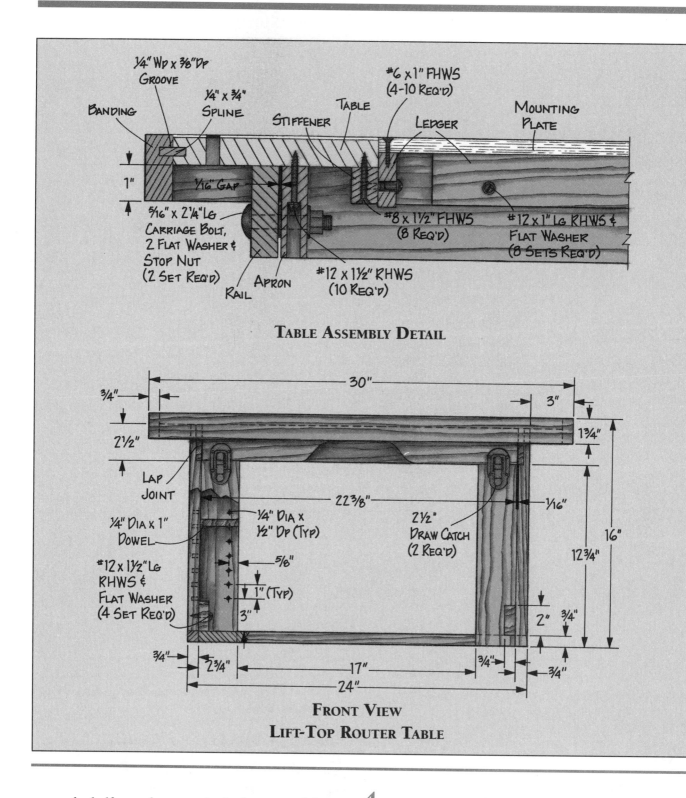

TABLE ASSEMBLY DETAIL

FRONT VIEW
LIFT-TOP ROUTER TABLE

create the half-round grooves in the bottoms of the shelves and trays, as shown in *Tray/Section A*.

Note: Do not drill the ⁵⁄₁₆-inch-diameter holes in the rails and back side legs yet. Wait until after you've assembled the base and the apron.

4 Cut the shapes of the base parts. Lay out the ¾-inch-wide, 2-inch-long notches in the front legs, as shown in the *Front View*. Also mark the profiles of the back side legs, as shown in the *Side View*; the rails, as shown in the *Side View* and *Right Side Rail Layout*; and

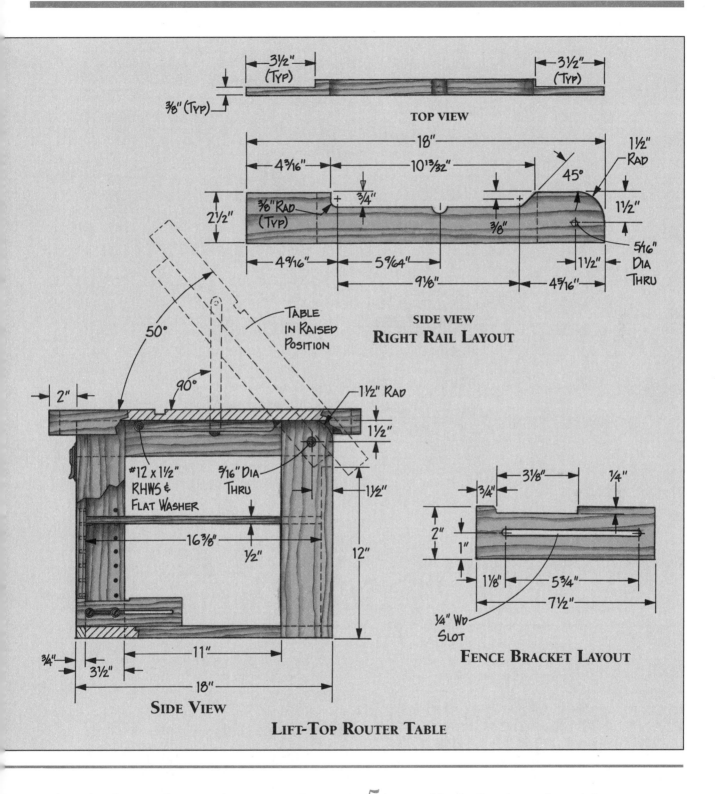

LIFT-TOP ROUTER TABLE

the fence brackets, as shown in the *Fence Bracket Layout*. Drill ¾-inch-diameter holes through the right rail to create the small radii in that profile. Cut the remaining shapes with a band saw, scroll saw, or saber saw. Sand the sawed edges.

5 Assemble the base. Finish sand the parts you have made, then glue the side legs and rails together. Let the glue dry, sand the lap joints clean and flush, then glue the front and back legs to the side leg assemblies. Let the glue dry again, and glue the leg

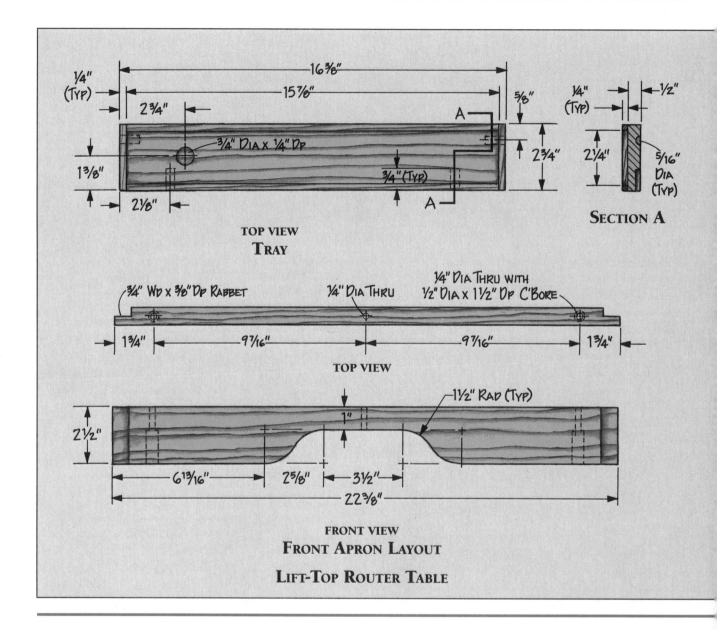

¼" (TYP)   2¾"   16⅜"   ⅝"   ¼" (TYP)   ½"

                                      15⅞"   A   2¾"   2¼"   5/16"
                                                                                              DIA
¾" DIA x ¼" DP   (TYP)
1⅜"

2⅛"   ¾"(TYP)   A   SECTION A

TOP VIEW
TRAY

¾" WD x ⅜" DP RABBET   ¼" DIA THRU   ¼" DIA THRU WITH
                                                   ½" DIA x 1½" DP C'BORE

1¾"   9⁷/16"   9⁷/16"   1¾"

TOP VIEW

                                        1"   —1½" RAD (TYP)
2½"

            6¹³/16"   2⅝"   3½"
                          22⅜"

FRONT VIEW
FRONT APRON LAYOUT

LIFT-TOP ROUTER TABLE

assemblies to the base. Attach the fence brackets to the side legs with roundhead wood screws and washers. Tighten the screws, then back them off ¼ turn so you can slide the fence brackets back and forth easily. When they are pushed all the way back, the front ends of the fence brackets should be flush with the front legs.

Measure the thickness of the base and the distance between the legs to calculate the sizes of the trim pieces. (They probably will have changed slightly from what is shown on the Materials List.) Cut the trim and glue it to the base.

Glue the trim on the trays. Insert the shelving support dowels in the stopped holes in the inside surfaces

of the legs and set the shelves and trays on them. The dowels should fit in the half-round grooves on the bottoms of these parts.

MAKING THE TABLE

6 Cut the joinery in the table parts. Cut the table parts to size, mitering the ends of the banding. Make the rabbets in the ends of the aprons, as shown in the *Front Apron Layout/Top View*. Rout the spline grooves in the edges of the table top and the inside faces of the banding, as shown in the *Table Assembly Detail*.

Lay out the slots and rabbets in the table, as shown in the *Top View*. Drill ⅞-inch-diameter access holes at

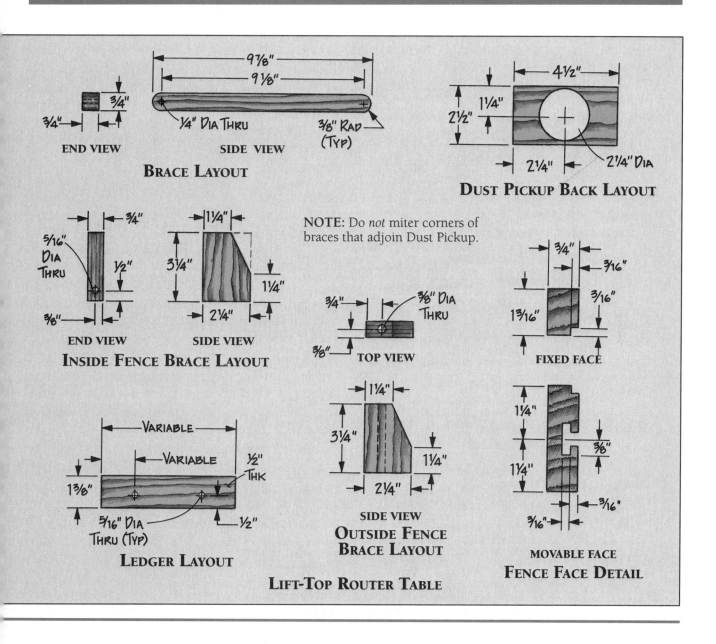

BRACE LAYOUT

END VIEW

SIDE VIEW

9⅞"

9⅛"

¾"

¾"

¼" DIA THRU

⅜" RAD (TYP)

DUST PICKUP BACK LAYOUT

4½"

1¼"

2½"

2¼"

2¼" DIA

NOTE: Do *not* miter corners of braces that adjoin Dust Pickup.

INSIDE FENCE BRACE LAYOUT

END VIEW

SIDE VIEW

¾"

1¼"

5/16" DIA THRU

½"

3¼"

⅜"

2¼"

1¼"

TOP VIEW

¾"

⅜" DIA THRU

⅜"

FIXED FACE

¾"

3/16"

3/16"

1 3/16"

LEDGER LAYOUT

VARIABLE

VARIABLE

½" THK

1⅜"

5/16" DIA THRU (TYP)

½"

OUTSIDE FENCE BRACE LAYOUT

SIDE VIEW

1¼"

3¼"

1¼"

2¼"

FENCE FACE DETAIL

MOVABLE FACE

1¼"

1¼"

⅜"

3/16"

3/16"

LIFT-TOP ROUTER TABLE

the front ends of the fence mounting slots. Rout the ⅜-inch-wide slots for the fence and the ½-inch-wide rabbets for the centering rules. Do *not* cut the miter gauge groove yet.

7 Install the mounting plate in the table. Cut the mounting plate to the size needed from ⅜-inch-thick clear acrylic plastic. (Do *not* use polycarbonates such as Lexan; they're too flexible.) Using a hole saw, cut a 2-inch-diameter access hole in the mounting plate for the router bits.

Lay out the position of the mounting plate on the bottom of the table. Attach the stiffeners to the table with glue and flathead wood screws, making sure the

mounting plate fits snugly between them. Use the stiffeners to guide a pattern-cutting bit (a straight bit with the guide bearing on top of the cutter), and rout the opening for the plate in the table. Square the corners with a flush-cut saw and a file.

Drill ⅝-inch-diameter holes through the ledgers, as shown in the *Ledger Layout,* and attach the ledgers to the stiffeners with roundhead wood screws and washers. Adjust the ledgers to hold the mounting plate flush with the table surface. (The oversize holes in the ledgers allow you to raise and lower them slightly.) Attach the mounting plate to the ledger with flathead wood screws.

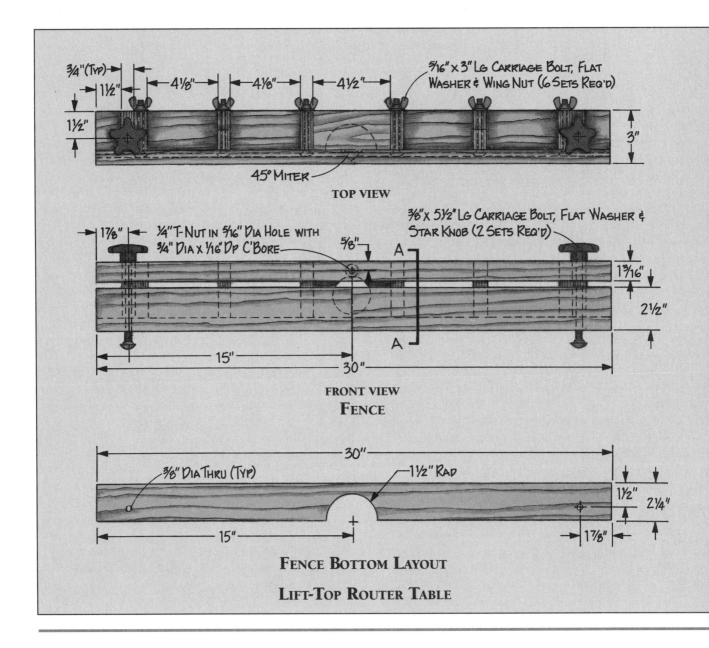

TOP VIEW

FRONT VIEW
FENCE

FENCE BOTTOM LAYOUT

LIFT-TOP ROUTER TABLE

8 Drill the holes in the table parts. Drill ¼-inch-diameter counterbored holes in the edges of the aprons to attach them to the table, as shown in the *Top View* and *Front Apron Layout/Top View*. Also drill a ¼-inch-diameter hole in the brace, as shown in the *Brace Layout/Side View*.

9 Cut the profiles of the table parts. Lay out the profiles of the front apron and the brace. Cut these profiles, then sand the sawed edges.

10 Assemble the table. Glue the banding to the table, using splines to reinforce the glue joints, as

shown in the *Table Assembly Detail*. Finish sand the aprons and glue them together. When the glue dries, position the apron assembly inside the legs on the base and clamp it in place. Drill ⁵⁄₁₆-inch-diameter pivot holes through the side legs and side aprons, as shown in the *Side View*. Also install the brace, attaching it to the right side apron with a roundhead wood screw and flat washer. Tighten the screw, then back it off ¼ turn so the brace swings freely.

Remove the apron assembly from the base and attach it to the bottom of the table with roundhead wood screws. Put the table in place on the base and attach it with carriage bolts, washers, and stop nuts

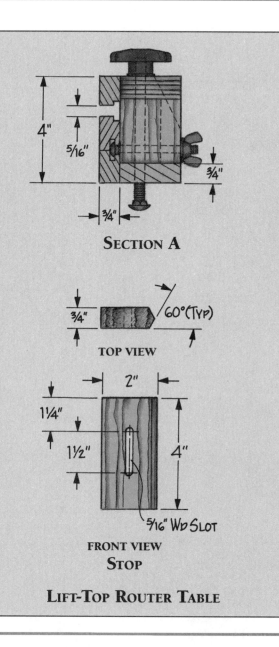

SECTION A

TOP VIEW

FRONT VIEW
STOP

LIFT-TOP ROUTER TABLE

■ ⅜-inch-diameter holes vertically through the two outside braces, as shown in the *Outside Fence Brace Layout/Top View*
■ ⅜-inch-diameter holes in the fence bottom, as shown in the *Fence Bottom Layout*
■ ⁵⁄₁₆-inch-diameter holes horizontally through the inside braces, as shown in the *Inside Fence Brace Layout/End View*
■ ⁵⁄₁₆-inch-diameter counterbored hole in the back of the fixed face (to hold a T-nut), as shown in the *Fence/Front View*

Using a hole saw, cut the 2¼-inch-diameter hole in the dust pickup back, as shown in the *Dust Pickup Back Layout.*

12 Cut the joinery in the fence parts. Cut the following joints in the faces, stops, and guard mount:
■ 2½-inch-wide, ⅛-inch-deep notch in the bottom end of the guard mount, as shown in the *Guard/Front View*
■ ½-inch-wide, ¹⁄₁₆-inch-deep rabbets in the guard mount, as shown in the *Guard/Bottom View*
■ ⁵⁄₁₆-inch-wide slots in the stops, as shown in the *Stop/Front View*
■ ¼-inch-wide slot in the guard mount
■ ³⁄₁₆-inch-wide, ³⁄₁₆-inch-deep rabbets in the top back edge of the top movable faces and the bottom back edge of the fixed face
■ ³⁄₁₆-inch-wide, ⅜-inch-deep grooves in the adjoining edges of the movable faces, as shown in the *Fence Face Details*

Cut the back sides of the grooves in the movable faces short so they form a T-slot when assembled.

13 Cut the shapes of the fence parts. Lay out the profiles of the fence bottom and the plastic guard, then cut them. Miter the corners of the fence braces, except for the two braces that adjoin the dust pickup, as shown in the *Inside Fence Brace Layout*. Double-miter one edge of each stop, as shown in the *Stop/ Top View*. Sand all sawed edges smooth.

14 Assemble the fence. Finish sand the wooden parts, then glue the braces, fence bottom, dust pickup top, and dust pickup back together. As you do so, insert carriage bolts through the holes in the fence bottom and the outside fence braces to help align them.

Glue the movable fence faces together, let the glue dry, then miter the inside ends, as shown in the *Fence/Top View*. Install a T-nut in the fixed face and glue the face to the fence braces. Attach the movable

through the pivot holes. Test the moving parts — when you lift up on the front edge of the table, the brace should swing down and rest in the half-round notch in the right rail. When you're satisfied the parts work properly, install the draw catches on the front legs and rout a slot in the table to fit your miter gauge.

MAKING THE FENCE

11 Drill the holes in the fence parts. Cut the fence parts to size, then drill:
■ ⅞-inch-diameter access hole in the guard mount, as shown in the *Guard/Front View*

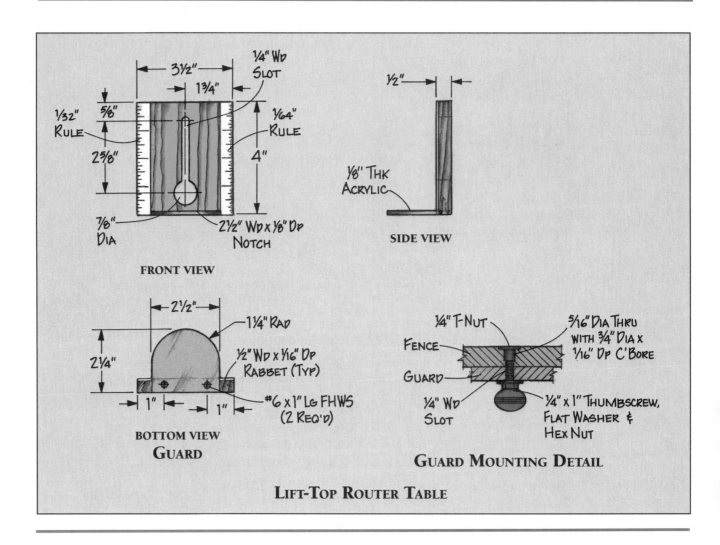

FRONT VIEW

SIDE VIEW

BOTTOM VIEW
GUARD

GUARD MOUNTING DETAIL

LIFT-TOP ROUTER TABLE

faces to the braces with carriage bolts, washers, and wing nuts. There should be a ⁵⁄₁₆-inch-wide gap between the fixed face and the movable faces — this lets you mount stops and other accessories to the fence. Tighten the hardware that holds the movable faces in place, then joint the faces perfectly straight and flat.

Cut the ¹⁄₃₂-inch and ¹⁄₆₄-inch rules to length (if necessary), then fasten them to the guard mount with epoxy cement. Fit the guard in the notch in the bottom of the guard mount and secure it with flathead wood screws. Attach the guard to the fence with a thumbscrew, hex nut, and flat washer, as shown in the *Guard Mounting Detail*. Attach the stops to the fence with carriage bolts, washers, and wing nuts.

Mount the completed fence on the table with carriage bolts, washers, and star knobs. Check that the fence slides smoothly in the table slots.

FINISHING UP

15 Finish the router table. Remove the fence from the table and the table from the base. Also remove the shelves and trays from the base. Disassemble the table and fence as much as possible and set the hardware aside. Apply a finish to all wooden surfaces. Let the finish dry, then reassemble the router table and fence.

16 Install the router and the centering rules.
Attach the router to the mounting plate. Install a pointed router bit (such as a V-groove cutter) in the router and adjust the depth of cut so the point is even with the top surface of the plate. Using a T-square or a straightedge, draw a line across the table parallel to the front edge that intersects the centering rule grooves and the point of the bit. Install the centering rules in the grooves, aligning the "0" marks with the line you drew.

9. ROUTER HEIGHT ADJUSTOR

When using a router, you must adjust the depth of cut frequently — many operations require you to change it before every pass. This can be frustrating because the mechanisms for raising and lowering a plunge router are not always easy to operate, nor are they especially precise. "Height adjustors" (which fit over the threaded posts on plunge routers) offer some relief, but they require quite a bit of wrist twisting.

This simple jig is the best solution I've come up with. It's a height adjustor with a crank attached to the top end, and it works with both portable (A) and table-mounted (B) plunge routers. The crank has a free-spinning handle, so there's no need for any wrist action. Just grab onto the handle and turn the crank, and the router moves up and down smoothly. To adjust the depth of cut in precise increments, simply count your turns. If you know the thread pitch on the post, you can easily figure how far the router travels with each turn. If the thread pitch is 16, for example, the router moves 1/16 inch with every turn.

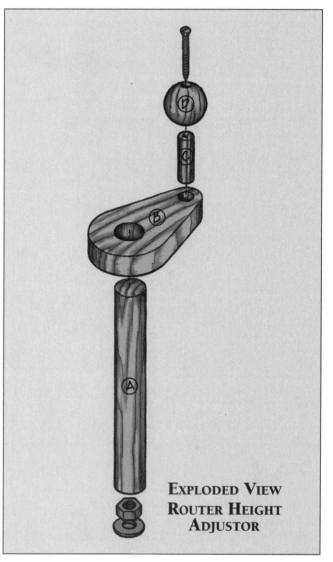

**EXPLODED VIEW
ROUTER HEIGHT
ADJUSTOR**

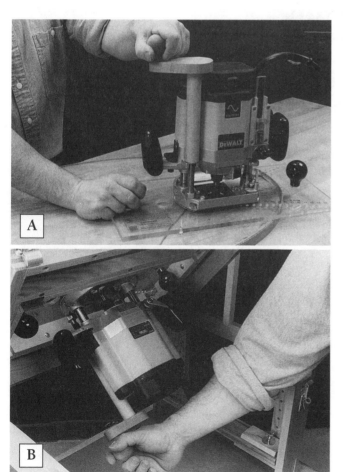

MATERIALS LIST (FINISHED DIMENSIONS)

Parts

A. Adjustment
   post   1″ dia. x (variable)
B. Crank arm   ¾″ x 2½″ x 4¼″
C. Handle post   ½″ dia. x 2″
D. Ball handle   1½″ dia.

Hardware

#8 x 1¾″ Ovalhead wood screw

Hex nut (to fit threaded post on
   router)

Flat washer (to fit threaded post
   on router)

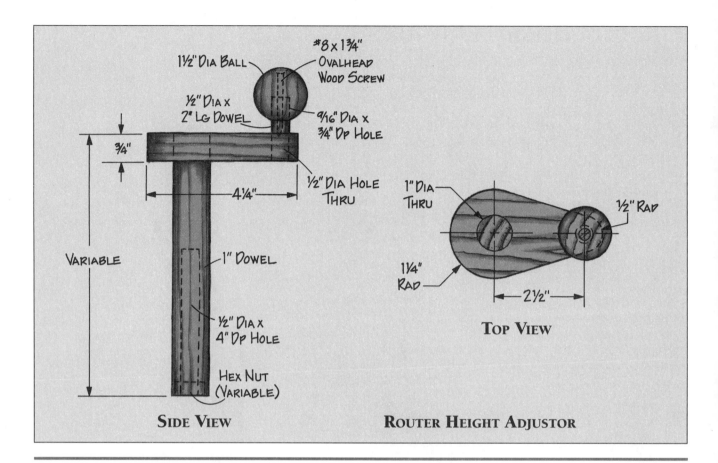

SIDE VIEW   **ROUTER HEIGHT ADJUSTOR**

PLAN OF PROCEDURE

1 Select the stock and cut the parts. Purchase the wooden ball you need to make this fixture from a crafts store or mail-order supplier of wooden parts. The other parts can be made from scraps of wood and dowels. On your router, measure the distance from the flanges or guides that fit around the threaded post to the top of the router body and add 1 inch — this is the length of the adjustment post. Cut the parts to size.

2 Drill the holes. Lay out the profile of the crank arm and the positions of the holes. Then drill:
■ 1-inch-diameter hole through the crank arm, as shown in the *Top View*
■ ⁹⁄₁₆-inch-diameter, ¾-inch-deep hole in the ball handle, as shown in the *Side View*
■ ½-inch-diameter hole through the crank arm
■ ½-inch-diameter, 4-inch-deep hole in the end of the adjustment post

3 Cut the profile of the crank arm. Cut the shape of the crank arm with a band saw, scroll saw, or saber saw. Sand the sawed surfaces smooth.

4 Assemble the router height adjustor. With a chisel, cut a recess in the bottom of the adjustment post to fit the hex nut. Install the hex nut in the post with epoxy cement.

Glue the adjustment post, crank arm, and handle post together. Slip the ball handle over the handle post and secure it with an ovalhead wood screw. Tighten the screw, then loosen it ¼ turn so the ball spins freely.

5 Finish the height adjustor. Remove the ball handle, do any necessary sanding, and apply a finish to all wooden surfaces. When the finish dries, replace the ball handle. As you do so, put a little epoxy cement in the screw hole in the handle post. When the cement dries, it will keep the screw from backing out.

Secure the height lock on your plunge router and remove the nuts and other hardware from the threaded post. Place a flat washer over the post, then install the height adjustor.

10. TILTING DRILL PRESS TABLE

A drill press is essential for accurate woodworking. Unfortunately, most presses are designed for metal-working and have some serious shortcomings in a woodworking shop. The most glaring problem is the table — it's too small, has no fence, and tilts in the wrong direction. Happily, this can be easily fixed — just build another table.

I designed this particular table to fit my benchtop drill press, but it will also fit most floor and radial models. It has a generous work surface, a movable fence, and it tilts up to 55 degrees front to back (*A*

and *B*). This gives it unlimited horizontal work capacity at any angle. Additionally:

■ The fence is slotted so you can mount stops and other accessories. The stops shown flip out of the way when you're not using them.

■ The fence stores directly underneath the table, where you can reach it easily (*C*).

■ The tilt mechanism doesn't limit the vertical travel of the table. Unlike ordinary table trunnions, which hang down, the braces fold up underneath the table so they won't reduce the work capacity of the tool.

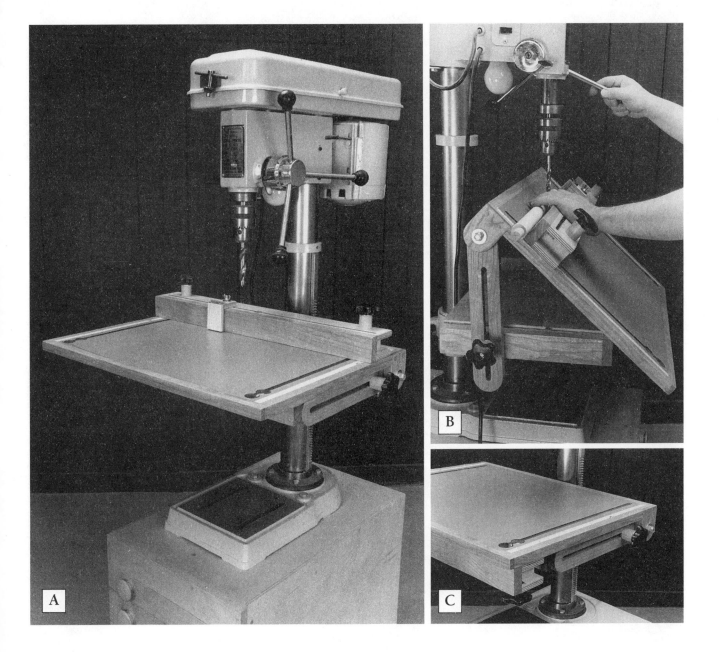

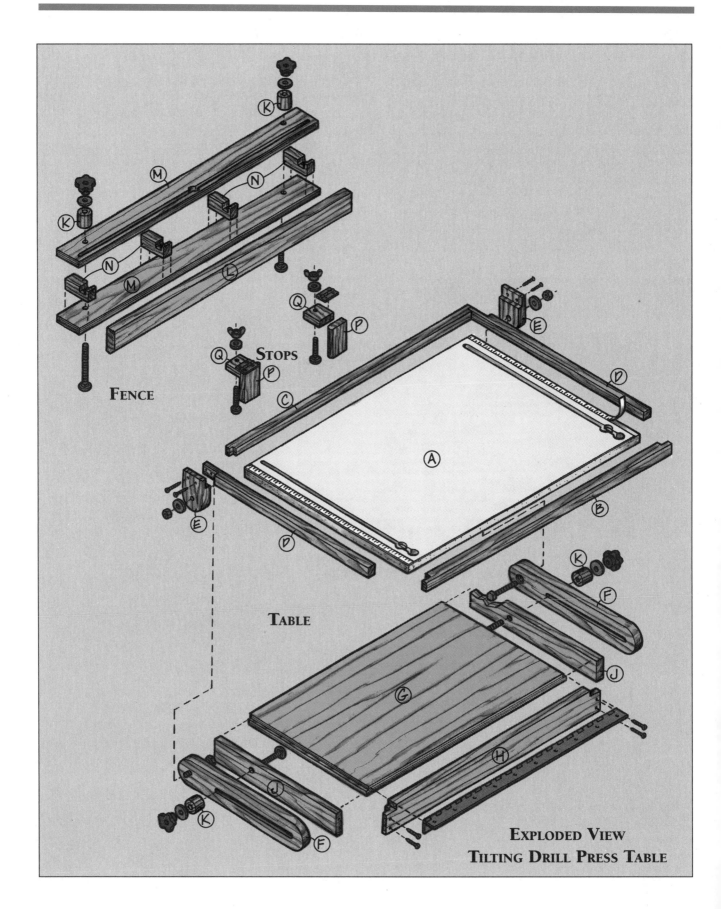

Fence

Stops

Table

Exploded View
Tilting Drill Press Table

MATERIALS LIST (FINISHED DIMENSIONS)

Parts

A. Table*   ¾" x 16½" x 22½"
B. Front trim   ¾" x ¾" x 24"
C. Back trim   ¾" x ¾" x 23¼"
D. Side trim (2)   ¾" x ¾" x 17¼"
E. Pivot blocks (2) ¾" x 2¼" x 3"
F. Braces (2)   ¾" x 2¼" x 12¾"
G. Mount†   ¾" x 12" x 19½"
H. Front apron   ¾" x 2¼" x 21"
J. Side aprons (2) ¾" x 2¼" x 12⅜"
K. Spacers (4)   1" dia. x 1"
L. Fence face   ¾" x 2" x 24"
M. Fence top/ bottom† ½" x 2¼" x 24"

N. Fence ribs (4) ¾" x 1" x 2¼"
P. Stops (2)   ½" x 1½" x 2⅜"
Q. Stop mounts (2) ½" x 1½" x 1⅝"

Hardware

#8 x 1¼" Flathead wood screws (8)
⅜" x 4½" Carriage bolts (2)
⅜" x 3" Carriage bolts (2)
⅜" x 2" Hex bolts (2)
¼" x 1½" Carriage bolts (2)
⅜" Flat washers (6)
¼" Flat washers (2)
⅜" Star knobs (4)

⅜" Stop nuts (2)
¼" Wing nuts (2)
1½" x 19" Piano hinge and mounting screws
1" x 1½" Butt hinges and mounting screws (2)
½" x 24" Self-stick centering rules (2)
Plastic laminate (19" x 25" sheet — optional)

*Make this part from medium-density fiberboard (MDF).
†Make these parts from plywood.

PLAN OF PROCEDURE

1 Select the stock and cut the parts. To make this drill press table, you need about 3 board feet of 4/4 (four-quarters) hardwood, an 18-inch-wide by 24-inch-long sheet of medium density fiberboard (MDF), some scraps of ¾-inch and ½-inch plywood, and a scrap of 1-inch-diameter dowel. Plane the 4/4 stock to ¾ inch thick and cut all the parts except the stops and stop mounts. For these parts, select a piece of ¾-inch-thick wood, plane it to ½ inch thick, then cut them to size.

If you wish, cover the top surface of the table with plastic laminate to make it more durable. You can also use a laminate-covered sink cutout to make the table. These are available at most lumberyards and building supply outlets.

2 Drill the holes and counterbores. Lay out the holes and counterbores in the table, pivot blocks, braces, apron sides, fence top, fence bottom, and stop mounts. Then drill:
- ⅞-inch-diameter access holes through the table, as shown in the *Top View*
- ⅞-inch-diameter counterbores in the top surface of the table
- ⅝-inch-diameter access hole through the fence top, as shown in the *Fence/Top View*
- ⅜-inch-diameter counterbored holes through the inside faces of the braces, as shown in the *Brace Layout*

- ⅜-inch-diameter holes in the pivot blocks, as shown in the *Side View*
- ⅜-inch-diameter holes in the side aprons, as shown in the *Mount Assembly*
- ⅜-inch-diameter holes through the fence top and bottom
- ⅜-inch-diameter holes through the spacers
- ¼-inch-diameter holes through the stop mount, as shown in the *Stop/Side View*

> ### TRY THIS TRICK
>
> **T**o save time and keep the fixture symmetrical, "pad drill" holes in identical parts. Tape the parts together face to face to make a pad, make sure the edges are flush, then drill through the entire pad.

3 Cut the joinery. Rout ⅜-inch-wide slots in the table, as shown in the *Top View*, and the braces, as shown in the *Brace Layout*. Rout a ¼-inch-wide slot in the fence top, as shown in the *Fence/Top View.*

Cut these interlocking rabbets, as shown in the *Top View* and *Mount Assembly:*
- 1⅞-inch-wide, ⅜-inch-deep rabbets in the back ends of the side trim

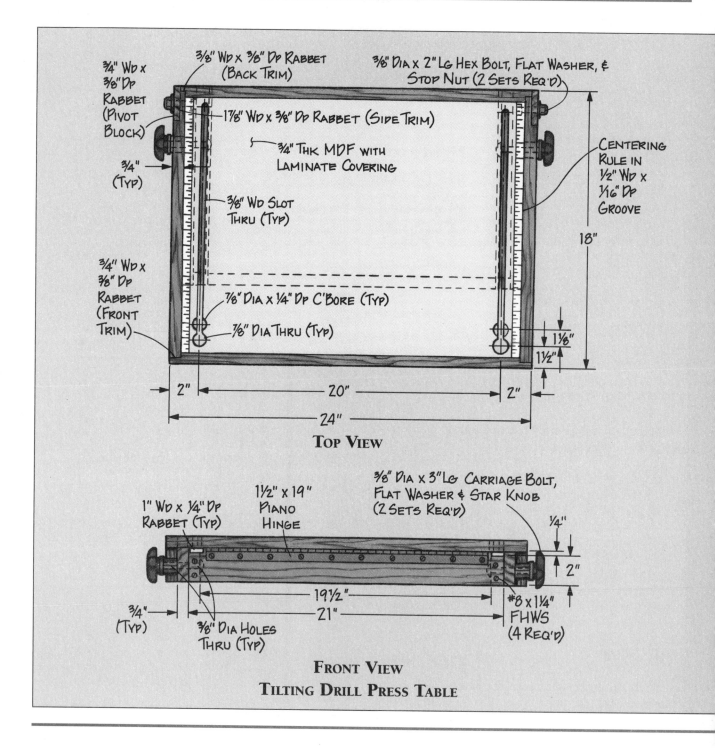

Top View

Front View
Tilting Drill Press Table

■ ¾-inch-wide, ⅜-inch-deep rabbets in the ends of the front trim, the front apron, and the top ends of the pivot blocks

■ ⅜-inch-wide, ⅜-inch-deep rabbets in the ends of the back trim

Also make ⅝-inch-wide notches in the top edges of the fence ribs, as shown in the *Fence Rib Layout.*

(These notches provide clearance for the heads of the carriage bolts that secure the stops to the fence.)

4 Cut the chamfers and profiles. Chamfer both corners on one edge of each stop, as shown in the *Stop/Top View,* and the bottom front corner of the fence face, as shown in the *Fence/End View.* Using a

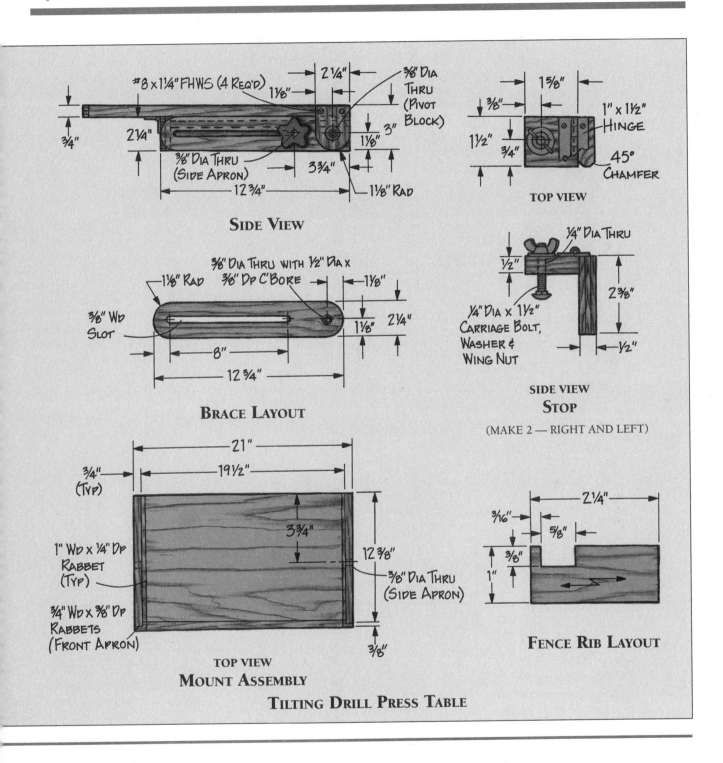

#8 x 1¼" FHWS (4 REQ'D)

⅜" DIA THRU (PIVOT BLOCK)

⅜" DIA THRU (SIDE APRON)

1⅛" RAD

SIDE VIEW

1" x 1½" HINGE

45° CHAMFER

TOP VIEW

⅜" DIA THRU WITH ½" DIA x ⅜" DP C'BORE

1⅛" RAD

⅜" WD SLOT

BRACE LAYOUT

¼" DIA THRU

¼" DIA x 1½" CARRIAGE BOLT, WASHER & WING NUT

SIDE VIEW
STOP
(MAKE 2 — RIGHT AND LEFT)

21"

19½"

¾" (TYP)

1" WD x ¼" DP RABBET (TYP)

¾" WD x ⅜" DP RABBETS (FRONT APRON)

3¾"

12⅜"

⅜" DIA THRU (SIDE APRON)

TOP VIEW
MOUNT ASSEMBLY

FENCE RIB LAYOUT

TILTING DRILL PRESS TABLE

band saw, scroll saw, or saber saw, round the bottom ends of the pivot blocks and both ends of the braces. Sand the sawed edges.

5 Assemble the table. Finish sand the table parts. Glue the table, trim, and pivot blocks together, reinforcing the joints that hold the pivot block to the table with flathead wood screws. Also glue the mount and aprons together and strengthen the corner joints with screws.

When the glue dries, cut 1-inch-wide, ¼-inch-deep rabbets in the top of the mount assembly, along both sides, as shown in the *Front View* and the *Mount Assembly*. (These rabbets provide clearance for the

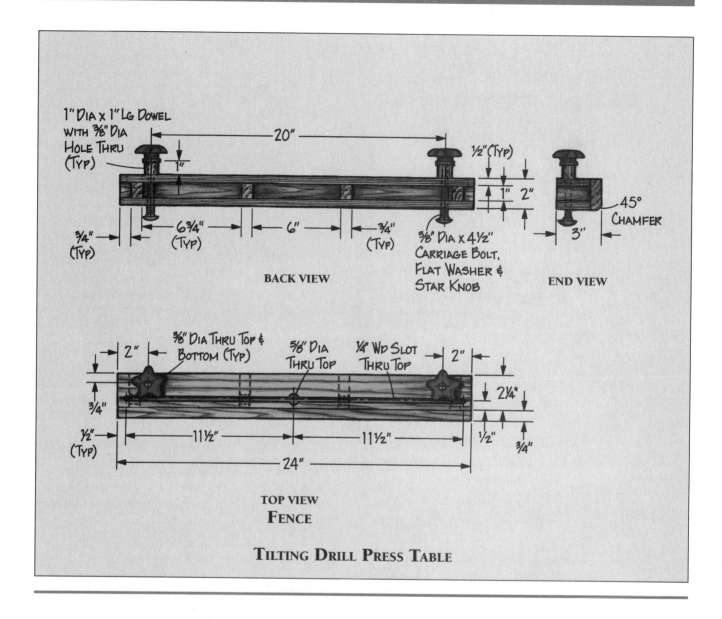

BACK VIEW

END VIEW

TOP VIEW
FENCE

TILTING DRILL PRESS TABLE

heads of the bolts that hold the fence to the table.) Be careful not the nick the screws.

Attach the table to the mount with a piano hinge. Drive the heads of the hex bolts into the counterbores in the braces and attach them to the pivot blocks with washers and stop nuts. Tighten the nuts, then back them off a fraction of a turn so the braces swing freely. Secure the braces to the side aprons with carriage bolts, spacers, washers, and star knobs.

Test the tilting action of the table. As you lift up on the back edge, the braces should unfold. Tighten the star knobs to lock the table at any angle.

6 Assemble the fences and stops. Finish sand the fence and stop parts. Glue the fence face, top,

bottom, and ribs together. When the glue dries, joint the fence face straight, flat, and square to the bottom. Attach the stops to the mounts with butt hinges.

Install the carriage bolts, spacers, washers, and star knobs in the fence, then check that the fence moves back and forth smoothly in the table slots. Install the carriage bolts, washers, and wing nuts in the stops, then check that they slide smoothly in the fence slot.

7 Finish the drill press table, fence, and stops. Disassemble the table, fence, and stops. Set the hardware aside and do any necessary touch-up sanding. Apply a finish to all wooden surfaces. Let the finish dry, then reassemble the project.

11. Circular Saw Guide

Like most craftsmen, I do a fair amount of work with plywood and other sheet materials. And like most, I've found it difficult to cut up full-size sheet goods with ordinary stationary power tools. Unfortunately, I don't do enough of this work to justify the expense of a panel saw, nor would I have room in my shop even if I did. So I devised this inexpensive, space-saving circular saw accessory.

This jig consists of two straightedges, each approximately 4 feet long, that guide the saw. Use them singly to cut across the width of a standard sheet (A), or join them end to end (B) to make a single, superlong guide to rip the full length (C). A wide base, custom-fit to your saw, helps position the straightedges accurately, and built-in clamps secure them to the sheet.

Surprisingly, this jig takes no more time to set up and use than a panel saw. And, as long as you use a sharp, high-quality blade in your circular saw, it's just as accurate.

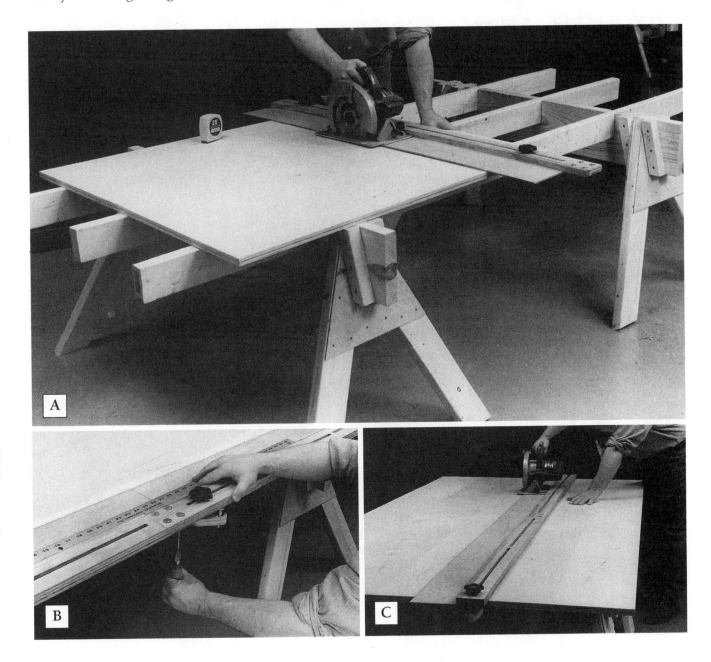

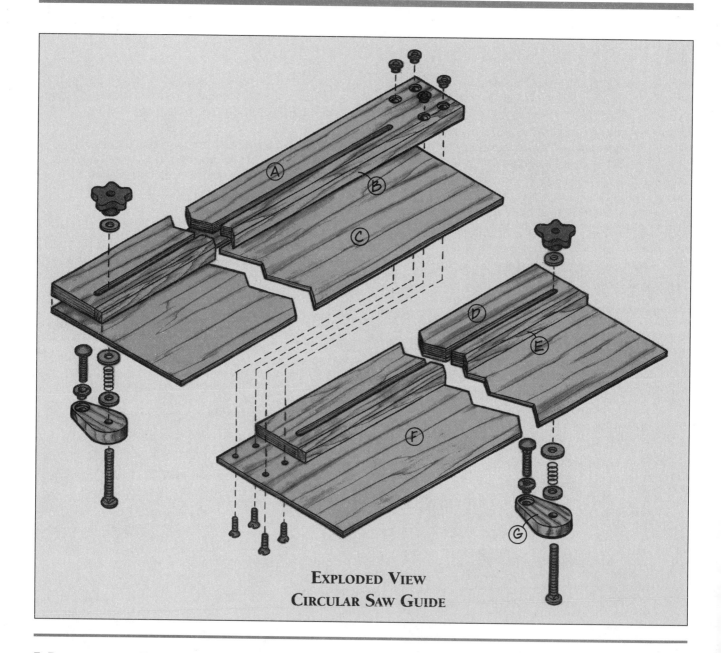

EXPLODED VIEW
CIRCULAR SAW GUIDE

MATERIALS LIST (FINISHED DIMENSIONS)

Parts

A. First guide*   ¾" x 3" x 55"
B. First guide trim ¾" x ¾" x 55"
C. First guide
    base*   ¼" x 11"† x 52"
D. Second guide* ¾" x 3" x 45"
E. Second guide
    trim   ¾" x ¾" x 45"
F. Second guide
    base*   ¼" x 11"† x 48"
G. Clamps (2)   ¾" x 2" x 3½"

Hardware

⅜" x 3" Carriage bolts (2)
⅜" x 2" Carriage bolts (2)
¼" x ¾" Flathead machine screws
  (4)
⅜" Flat washers (4)
⅜" Star knobs (2)
⅜" T-nuts (2)
¼" T-nuts (4)
⅜ I.D. x 1½" Compression springs
  (2)

Make these parts from plywood.
†*Trim to final width after assembly.*

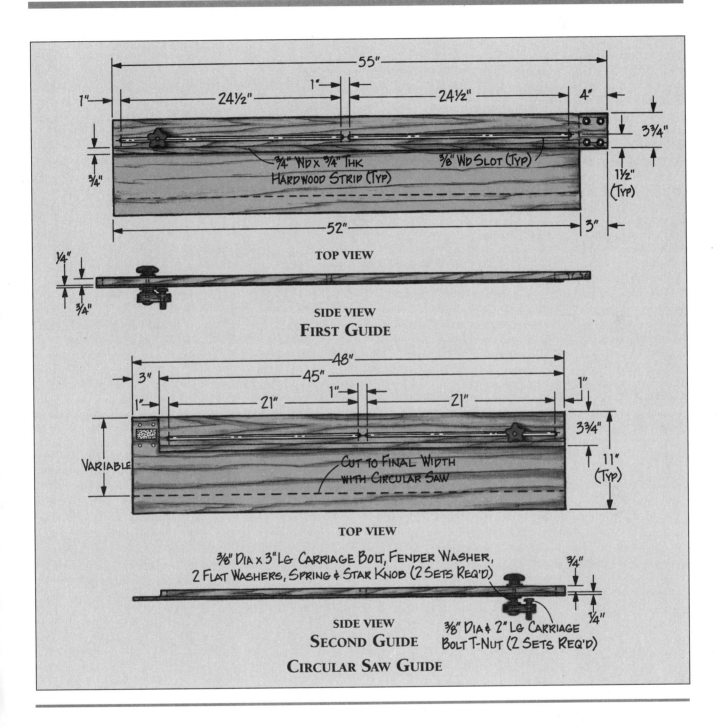

55"

1" 24½" 1" 24½" 4"

¾" Wd x ¾" Thk Hardwood Strip (Typ) ⅜" Wd Slot (Typ)

3¾"

1½" (Typ)

¾"

52" 3"

TOP VIEW

¼"

¾"

SIDE VIEW
FIRST GUIDE

48"

45"

3" 1" 21"

1"

21"

1"

3¾"

Variable

Cut to Final Width with Circular Saw

11" (Typ)

TOP VIEW

⅜" Dia x 3" Lg Carriage Bolt, Fender Washer, 2 Flat Washers, Spring & Star Knob (2 Sets Req'd)

¾"

¼"

SIDE VIEW
SECOND GUIDE

⅜" Dia & 2" Lg Carriage Bolt T-Nut (2 Sets Req'd)

CIRCULAR SAW GUIDE

Plan of Procedure

1 Select the stock and cut the parts. To make this circular saw guide, you need a 7-inch-wide by 60-inch-long piece of ¾-inch plywood, a 24-inch-wide by 60-inch-long piece of ¼-inch plywood, and some long scraps of ¾-inch-thick hardwood. Cut the clamps and the guide bases to size, but make the guides and the trim about an inch longer than specified.

2 Assemble the guides. Let these parts "shop dry" for several days to equalize their moisture content. (This helps prevent the assembled guides from bowing.) Glue the hardwood trim to the guides, let the glue dry, then cut them to length. Joint the hardwood edge straight. **Note:** Do *not* try to joint plywood. The glue between the plies will ruin the jointer knives.

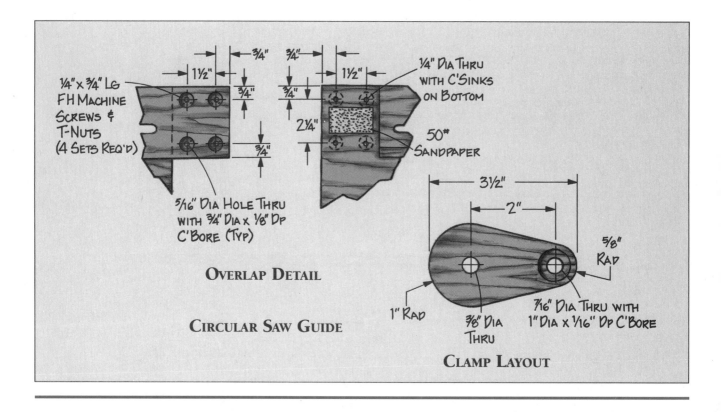

¼" x ¾" LG FH MACHINE SCREWS & T-NUTS (4 SETS REQ'D)

¼" DIA THRU WITH C'SINKS ON BOTTOM

50# SANDPAPER

5/16" DIA HOLE THRU WITH ¾" DIA x ⅛" DP C'BORE (TYP)

OVERLAP DETAIL

CIRCULAR SAW GUIDE

3½"

2"

5/8" RAD

1" RAD

⅜" DIA THRU

7/16" DIA THRU WITH 1" DIA x 1/16" DP C'BORE

CLAMP LAYOUT

Glue each guide to its base, making sure the back edges are flush. The first guide should overlap its base by 3 inches, while the second should be 3 inches shorter than its base, as shown in the *First Guide/Top View* and *Second Guide/Top View.*

3 Drill the holes. Lay out the holes and slots in the guides and the clamps. Temporarily clamp the guides together so the first guide overlaps the base of the second. Make sure the edges are aligned perfectly straight. Drill ¼-inch-diameter holes through the parts where they overlap, as shown in the *Overlap Detail.*

Take the guides apart. Counterbore the holes on the top surface of the first guide and countersink the holes on the bottom surface of the second guide base.

Also drill ⅜-inch-diameter holes and 7/16-inch-diameter counterbored holes in the clamps, as shown in the *Clamp Layout.*

4 Rout the slots. Rout ⅜-inch-wide slots in the guides, as shown in the *First Guide/Top View* and *Second Guide/Top View.*

5 Cut the clamp profiles. Using a band saw, scroll saw, or saber saw, cut the profiles of the clamps. Sand the sawed edges.

6 Trim the guide bases. Install the T-nuts in the counterbores in the first guide, then join the guides with machine screws. Again, make sure the edges are aligned perfectly straight. Install T-nuts, carriage bolts, washers, and springs in the clamps, then attach the clamps to the guides.

Fasten the guides to an 8-foot-long piece of plywood or particleboard with the clamps. Use the large end of each clamp as the jaw. Adjust the carriage bolt in the small end to keep the jaw from tipping when you tighten the star knob.

Rest your circular saw on one of the bases with the motor pointing toward the guide. Keeping the sole of the saw against the guides, trim the bases. Thereafter, you can use the edges of the bases to align the guides with the layout lines, *provided you always use the same circular saw and the same blade.*

7 Finish the saw guide. Remove the clamps from the guides and set the hardware aside. Do any necessary sanding and apply a finish. When the finish dries, reassemble the guides and clamps. Glue a small piece of coarse sandpaper to the second guide base, as shown in the *Overlap Detail.* This will help keep the guides aligned when they are joined. (**Note:** When joining the guides, always use a straightedge to help align them.)

12. KNOCK-DOWN CUTTING GRID

Although I still refer to it as a cutting grid, this fixture does so much more. It was originally intended as the other half of my cutting system for sheet materials. The sawhorses and rails form a grid that supports both the length and the width of the sheets while you saw them (*A*). Set your saw so it just barely cuts through the stock. (The blade will bite into the grid slightly, but this won't affect its usefulness.) The sheet remains perfectly flat during the cut; pieces don't sag or drop to the floor. And when you've finished cutting, the grid knocks down and stores against a wall (*B*).

After building it, however, I found many additional uses. It's an excellent assembly stand, clamping grid, finishing rack, and auxiliary workbench. If you do much finish carpentry, it's great for handling drywall and paneling. In fact, it's so functional that it spends more time set up than it does knocked down.

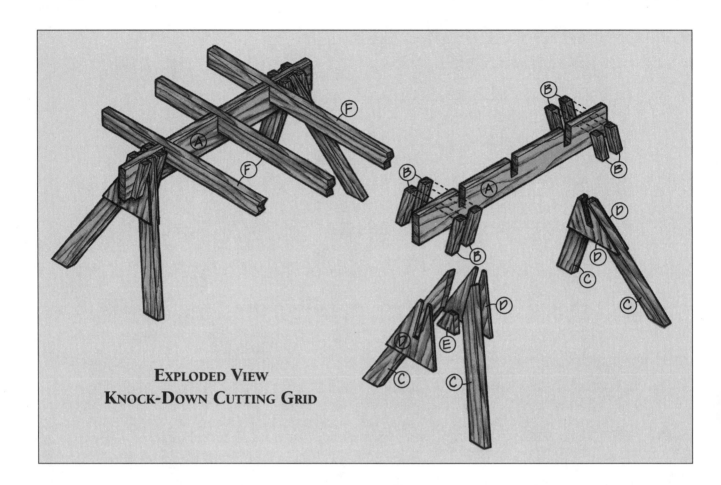

EXPLODED VIEW
KNOCK-DOWN CUTTING GRID

MATERIALS LIST (FINISHED DIMENSIONS)

Parts

A. Supports
   (2)   1½" x 7¼" x 47⅞"
B. Cleats (16)   1½" x 1½" x 8"
C. Legs (8)   1½" x 3½" x 28⅞"
D. Gussets (8)*   ¼" x 12" x 13½"
E. Spacers (4)   1½" x 3½" x 5¼"
F. Rails (3)   1½" x 3½" x 96"

Hardware

4d Common nails (72–84)
10d Common nails (24–30)

* Make these parts from plywood.

PLAN OF PROCEDURE

1 Select the stock and cut the parts. To make the cutting grid, you need a two-by-eight, 8 feet long; 7 straight two-by-fours, each 8 feet long; and a 24-inch-wide by 48-inch-long sheet of ¼-inch plywood. Cut the parts to size, mitering the ends of the legs and the edges of the gussets, as shown in the *Leg Assembly/Front View,* and the ends of the cleats, as shown in the *Support Layout/Side View.*

2 Cut the notches in the supports and gussets. Create 1⅝-inch-wide, 3½-inch-deep notches in the supports, as shown in the *Support Layout/Side View.* Cut the sides of the notches with a hand saw or saber saw, then remove the waste and cut the bottoms flat with a wide chisel. Also cut 1½-inch-wide, 7½-inch-deep notches in the gussets, as shown in the *Leg Assembly/Front View.*

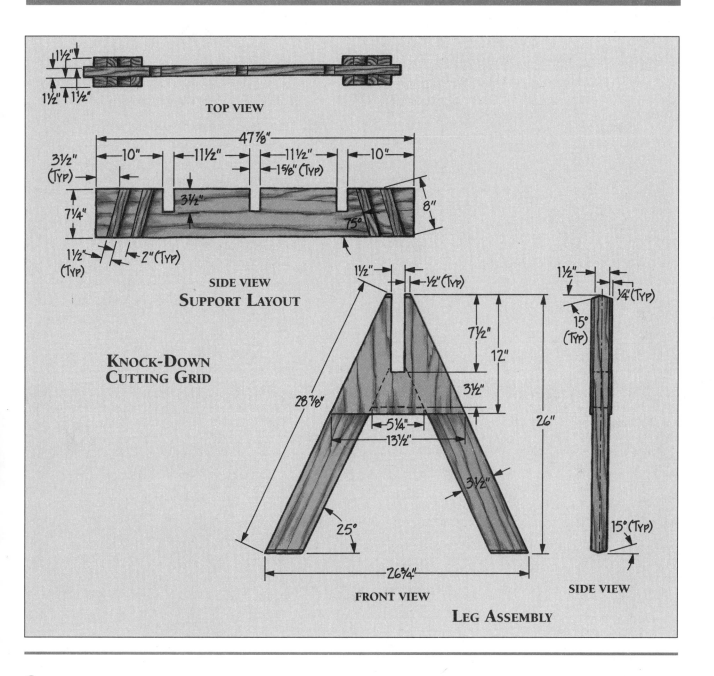

KNOCK-DOWN CUTTING GRID

TOP VIEW

SUPPORT LAYOUT

SIDE VIEW

LEG ASSEMBLY

FRONT VIEW

SIDE VIEW

3 Assemble the legs and supports. Join the legs, spacers, and gussets with 4d nails and waterproof glue (in case you use this fixture outside). To help keep the legs and spacers aligned while you attach the gussets, build an assembly jig to hold them — nail small blocks to a scrap of plywood, arranging the blocks to hold the parts in the proper configuration. Place the parts between the blocks. After attaching the first gusset to its legs and spacer, lift the assembly out of the jig, turn it over, and attach the second gusset.

Attach the cleats to the supports with 10d nails. *Don't* glue these parts together — if you do, the cleats will prevent the supports from expanding and contracting, eventually causing the supports to split.

4 Miter the ends of the legs. With a circular saw or a saber saw, double-miter both ends of each leg, as shown on the *Side View.*

5 Assemble the grid. To set up the grid, slide the leg assemblies between the cleats on the supports. Arrange the assembled sawhorses so the supports are roughly parallel and 4 to 6 feet apart, then rest the rails in the support notches.

INDEX

Note: Page references in *italic* indicate photographs or illustrations. **Boldface** references indicate charts or tables.

A–E

Assembly jigs, 59, *59*, 60, *60*
Auxiliary fence, *65–68*, 69, 72
Band saw, *21*, 22, 23, 34, *44*, 64, 70, 72, 77, 80, 88, 120
Bevel-setting jig, *41*
Calipers, 40, *40*
Cam clamp, *51*
Center finder, *41*
Circle-sanding jig, *35*
Circular saw guide, *62*, *117–120*
Clamp bar, *50*
Clamping grid, *62*, *62*, 121
Clamps, 10, *10*, **11**, *20*, 47–54, *48–56*, 58, 59, *59*, 60, *60*, 84–86, *87*, 88, *88*, 118–120, *120*
Corner
  bracket, *14*
  clamp, 59, *59*, 60
  jig, 59, *60*
Drill guide, 37, *37*
Drill press
  dust pickup, 23
  fence, *5*, *33*, 42, *42*, 43, 45, *111–116*
  tilting table, *30*, *41*, *62*, *111–116*
Drum sanding jig, *24*
Dust collection, 6, 18, 22, *22*, 23, 24, *24*, *25*, 26, *26*, 29, 32, *32*, 43, 44, 98, 100, *105*, 107
Expander, *50*

F–J

Featherboard, 20, *20*, *21*, 32, *62*, 65, 69–72
Fence, 4, *4*, *5*, **8**, *12*, *15*, *17*, *21*, 27, 31, 32, *32–34*, 38, *39*, 42, *42*, 43, *43*, *62*, *65–68*, 69, 72, *80–83*, 84, 86, 98–101, 103–108, *111–116*
Finger jig, *45*
Fluting jig, *58*
Guidance, 27, 32–37, *32–37*
Height-adjustment fence, *62*, *80–83*
Hold-down, 10, **11**, *21*, 47, 53–57
Holding jig, 57, *57*, 58, *58*
Honing guide, *49*
Incremental positioning jig, *46*
Jointer, *21*, *25*, *33*, 44, 64, 73
Jointing jig, *5*, 34

K–N

Knock-down cutting grid, *62*, *121–123*
L-beam fence, 32, *33*
Levers, 52, *52*, 53, *53*
Long-reach C-clamp, *49*, 53
Making jigs and fixtures
  common assemblies, **11**
  construction methods, 4, 7, 12, 13, *13*, 14, *14*, *15*, 43
  counterbores, 15, *15–17*, 34, 68, 71, 82, 83, 88, *92–94*, 95, 96, *96*, 97, 113, *114*, *115*, 120, *120*

designing, 3–6, *3–6*
  guard, *5*, *5*, **8**, 9, 91, 94–96, *97*, 100, 107, *108*
  guide bushing, **11**, 12, 35, *36*, 37, *37*
  hardware, 9, 10, *10*, **11**, 12, 66, 70, 75, 81, 85, 91, 100, 109, 113, 118, 122
  holes, 15, *15*, *16*, 34, 37, *37*, 96, 101, 113, 120
  materials, 7, **8**, 9, 13, 28–30, *28*, *29*, 64, 66, 70, 75, 81, 85, 91, 100, 109, 113, 118, 122
  pivot, 10, **11**, 12, 15, *16*, 30, *30*, 34, 35, 87, 89, 96, 97, 107, 113–115
  rolling surface, 30, 31, *31*
  sliding surface, 30, *30*, 31, *31*
  slots, 12, 15, *16*, *17*, *30*, 34, 65, 68, 71, 73, 75, 81, 82, 84, 87, 88, 91, 96–98, 107, 108, *108*, 113, *114*, 116, 120
  support, 27–31, *28–31*
  tilting surface, 30, *30*
  work surface, 7, **8**, 9, 27–30, *28–30*
Miter assembly jig, *59*
Miter gauge extension, *6*, 38
Mortising fence, *42*
Mortising template, 27, *36*
Notch jig, 58, *58*

P–T

Pattern, 7, **8**, 27, 34, 35, *36*
Pipe clamp rack, *29*
Planing jig, *48*
Preacher, *41*
Push
  block, 19, *19*, 20
  shoe, 19, *19*, 63
  stick, 19, *19*, 63
Pusher, 19, *62–64*
Radial arm saw, *25*, 38, *42*, 44
Router, 3, 4, *16*, *17*, 27, 28–30, 32, 33, 34, 35, 42, *42*, *48*, 58, 66, 98, 108, 109, 110
  compass jig, *17*, 34, 88, 96
  height adjustor, *62*, *109*, 110
  jack, *46*
Router table, 4, *21*, 22, *22*, 27, 33, 34, *39*, 42, 44, 46
  fence, *17*, *21*, 27, 33, 34, 38, *39*, 81, 98–101, 103–108
  lift-top, *21*, *30*, *62*, *98–108*
Routing jig
  horizontal, *29*
  multipurpose, *4*
  overhead, *3*
Safety, 2, 3, 5, *5*, 6, *6*, 18–21, *19–21*, 73
Sander, *14*, *23*, *29*, 34, 35
Screw clamp, *48*, *49*
Shave horse, 53, *53*
Slide rule, *39*, 40
Sliding
  cutoff table, *62*, *89–97*

miter table, 31
  table, 12, *21*, 29, 31, *39*, 43
Slope gauge, *41*
Small-parts handler, 19, *20*
Splined miter jig, *5*
Square-corner sanding jig, *15*
Stop, 4, *5*, 32, *33*, 38, 42, *42*, 43, *43–45*, *59*, 65, 66, 68, 91, *96*, 98, 100, 107, *107*, 111, *112*, 113, 114, *115*, 116
Storystick, 39, *39*, 40
Straightedge, 31, 32, *32*, 33, 34, *34*, *41*, 42, *43*, *50*, 84
Strap hold-down, *57*
Support, 27–31, *28–31*
Support stand, *31*, 44, *62*, *73–79*
T-square routing guide, 32
Table saw, *5*, 13, *13*, 19, *21*, *25*, 27, *31*, 38, 42, 43, 44, 64, 81, 89, 97
Tapering jig, *6*, 19
Techniques
  circles, 34, *35*, 73
  clamping, 10, **11**, *14*, 20, 29, 47–54, *48–56*, 57, 59, *59*, 60, *60*
  contours and curves, 34, *35*
  drilling, *15*, *23*, 27, *30*, 35, 37, *37*, *41*, 80, 110
  grinding, *30*, 33
  holding, 10, **11**, 47, 53, 55, 56, 57, *57*, 58, *58*
  jointing, *5*, 19, 34, 80
  layout, 39, *39*, 40, *40*, *41*
  marking, 40, *40*, *41*
  measuring, 38–40, *39–41*
  mortising, 27, *36*, 42
  planing, 19, *48*
  positioning, 38, 42, *42*, 43, *43*, 44, 45, *45*, 46
  routing, 3–5, 27, 29, 32, 33, 35, *36*, 68
  sanding, *15*, *24*, 27, 29, 33, 35
  sawing, *21*, 43
  tapering, *6*, 19
  turning, 57, *57*, 58, *58*
Template, **8**, 9, 27, 35, *36*
Tenoning jig, 19, *62*, *84–88*
Torsion box, 28, *28*, 29

U–W

V-jig, 57, *57*
Vacuum
  bag, 56
  clamps, 54, *54–56*
  hold-down, *20*, *54–56*
  hookup, 22, 23, *24*, *24*, 25
Violin clamp, *48*, 49
Wedge, 40, *41*, 48, *48*, 51, 58
Worktable extension, *73*, 75, 77, 78, 79

WOODWORKING GLOSSARY

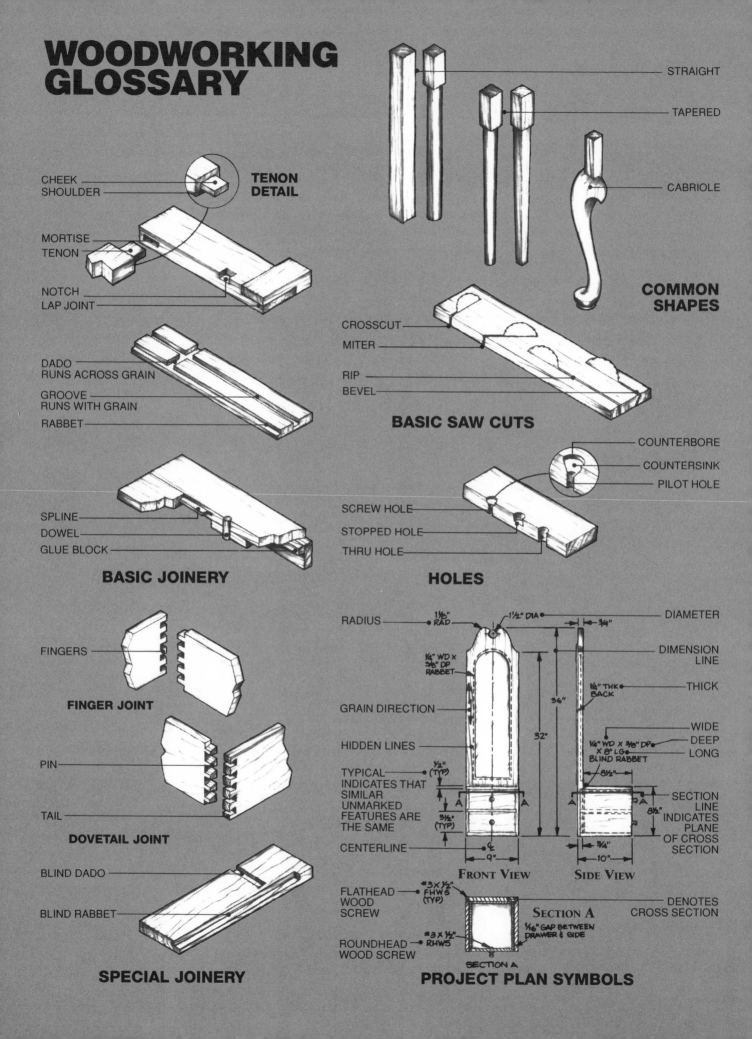

TENON DETAIL
CHEEK
SHOULDER

MORTISE
TENON

NOTCH
LAP JOINT

DADO
RUNS ACROSS GRAIN

GROOVE
RUNS WITH GRAIN

RABBET

BASIC JOINERY
SPLINE
DOWEL
GLUE BLOCK

FINGER JOINT
FINGERS

DOVETAIL JOINT
PIN
TAIL

SPECIAL JOINERY
BLIND DADO
BLIND RABBET

COMMON SHAPES
STRAIGHT
TAPERED
CABRIOLE

BASIC SAW CUTS
CROSSCUT
MITER
RIP
BEVEL

HOLES
COUNTERBORE
COUNTERSINK
PILOT HOLE
SCREW HOLE
STOPPED HOLE
THRU HOLE

RADIUS — 1⅛" RAD
1½" DIA — DIAMETER
¾"
¼" WD X ⅜" DP RABBET
DIMENSION LINE
¼" THK BACK — THICK
36"
32"
GRAIN DIRECTION
HIDDEN LINES
¼" WD X ⅜" DP X 8" LG BLIND RABBET
WIDE
DEEP
LONG
8½"
TYPICAL INDICATES THAT SIMILAR UNMARKED FEATURES ARE THE SAME
½" (TYP)
3½" (TYP)
A   A
A   A
8½"
SECTION LINE INDICATES PLANE OF CROSS SECTION
CENTERLINE
¢
9"
¾"
10"
FRONT VIEW   **SIDE VIEW**

FLATHEAD WOOD SCREW
#3 X ½" FHWS (TYP)
SECTION A
1/16" GAP BETWEEN DRAWER & SIDE
DENOTES CROSS SECTION
ROUNDHEAD WOOD SCREW
#3 X ½" RHWS
SECTION A

PROJECT PLAN SYMBOLS